Text copyright © 2020 by Ruth Bardis
Photographs copyright © 2020 by Ruth Bardis
Photography: Ruth Bardis
Styling: Ruth Bardis
Editor: Elite Authors
Graphic design: Kim Ellis
All rights reserved. This book or any portion thereof may not be reproduced or used in any manner whatsoever without the express written permission of the publisher.
ISBN: 978-0-646-81273-1

Acknowledgments

My heartfelt acknowledgment first and foremost goes to the people who encouraged me to write a second cookbook. The amazing response I received after my initial launch of *Hellenic Kanella* was a great factor as to why this book has come about. Thank you to those who trusted me yet again to research, develop, photograph, food-style, and document more recipes that encapsulate Greece.

To my parents, who loved the idea and believed in this project. Dad, thank you for the support you gave me to get this done, knowing again that I could do it better than the first time. To my extended family, siblings, nieces, and nephews, thank you for the excitement and for the testing of many recipes as they were being developed.

To my editors at Elite Authors – thank you!

To my nephew James, for giving me rights to some of your amazing Greece photos.

Tony Likousis, you deserve a noting here- thank you for being excited about this project, always asking me how things were progressing and excited for me to be undertaking such a task for the second time!

To my wonderful friend and graphic designer, Kim Ellis. You exceeded what I had hoped this book would look like. Thank you for coming along for the ride.

And finally, to the man behind this whole project, Athanasios! Your name should really be on the cover of this book! You are the driving force behind this adventure, spurring me on to do what I enjoy. Thank you for being my greatest supporter, engaging in this together! I love you!

About The Author

Ruth was born in Australia to Greek parents. Her strong ethnic heritage and love of nourishing food facilitated her switch from fashion designing to cooking, photography, and writing. Passionate about traditional Greek cuisine, she set off to learn extensively about her heritage, travelling countless times to Greece and revisiting her origins. She has lived in Greece, in America, and now resides in Australia.

Cook's Notes

Cooking Temperatures and Times

All recipes were tested on a gas stovetop and on a conventional fan-forced electric oven. You may need to adjust temperatures and cooking time if using an electric induction cooktop or a non-fan-forced oven.

Measurements

All cup measurements in this book use the American cup, which is slightly smaller than a metric cup.

1 cup = 240 mL
1/2 cup = 118 mL
1/3 cup = 79 mL
1 tablespoon = 15 mL
1 teaspoon = 5 mL

Produce and Ingredients

Unless otherwise stated, all recipes use the following:
Extra-virgin olive oil
Brown onions
Minced beef = ground beef
Red or green capsicums = bell peppers
Yogurt is always Greek yogurt
Full cream (whole) milk
Spring onion = green onion
Honey is always Greek honey

Cheese-Stuffed Veal in Tomato Sauce, 25
Chicken "Pollo in umido", 43
Dakos Salad, 151
Fish Soup with Saffron and White Wine, 167
Roast Beef with Vegetables and Melted Cheese, 195
Soup with Trahana, 201
Souvlaki, 224
Spicy Stew of Peppers, Sausage, and White Wine, 207
Stewed Aromatic Beef with Eggplant Mash, 65
Tomato Fritters from Santorini, 165
Venetian Pastitsio, 33
TRAHANA:
Cornmeal Spinach Pie with No Pastry, 197
Soup with Trahana, 201
Tomato Fritters from Santorini, 165
Trahana Pie with No Pastry, 203
Tzatziki (Yogurt and Garlic Sauce), 223

V

Vanilla Pastries, 145
VEAL:
Cheese-Stuffed Veal in Tomato Sauce, 25
Venetian Pastitsio, 33
VINEGAR:
Marinated Octopus, 229
Pickled Hot Peppers, 57

W

WALNUTS:
Beetroot Salad with Walnut, Apple, Honey, and Yogurt, 225
Chocolate and Walnut Cake, 111
Fried Pastry with Walnuts, Cinnamon, and Honey, 81
Grape Must Pudding, 93

Sesame Pie, 213
Spiced Tahini Baklava, 233
Spiced Walnut Cake with a Vanilla Custard Topping, 209
WHITE FISH:
Fish in Spicy Broth, 39
White Fish with Lemon Emulsion, 225
Wild Weeds with Lemon and Olive Oil, 157
WINE, RED:
Grilled Octopus, 182
Venetian Pastitsio, 33
WINE, WHITE:
Braised Artichokes with Baby Peas, 103
Cheese-Stuffed Veal in Tomato Sauce, 25
Chicken and Chickpea Stew, 175
Chicken "Pollo in umido", 43
Fish Soup with Saffron and White Wine, 167
Fried Snails with Rosemary, 147
Grilled Octopus, 182
Pork and Celery Stew with an Egg and Lemon Emulsion, 99
Spicy Stew of Peppers, Sausage, and White Wine, 207
Stewed Chicken with Sage and Rosemary, 154
Wine-Cooked Rooster with Egg Pasta, 87

Y

YOGURT:
Beetroot Salad with Walnut, Apple, Honey, and Yogurt, 225
Ice Cream Two Ways—Yogurt or Halva, 241
Revani (Yogurt and Semolina Cake), 69
Spiced Meatballs in a Lemon Yogurt Sauce, 125
Tzatziki (Yogurt and Garlic Sauce), 223
Yogurt-Coated Pasta with Caramelized Onions and Cheese, 179

To Athanasios

THERE IS NO ME, WITHOUT YOU...
THE HEART, FOLLOWING EVERY MEAL I MAKE,
AND THE GREATEST EARTHLY GIFT I POSSESS!

Just Some More

Nostalgia is an emotion that can come from many things and places: the scent of a candle, the pages of a new book, a bouquet of roses, or the smell of a classroom, to name a few. Nevertheless, the nostalgia one feels when a window is left open, wind blowing, with the gentle smell of a meal cooking away on the stove or in the oven from a neighboring home, when it gently hits your face, is captivating! Memories flood the mind as events are replayed, no matter how many years go by from one's childhood! You hear sounds of neighboring children, see vivid pictures of neighbors, and remember sounds that identify with that place. Isn't history amazing, that although we may not have lived through this place and time, we recollect stories told by our ancestors and envision pictures in our minds? How many of us have heard stories of war and hardship in the lives of our grandparents? And yet they withstood and lived long lives, and many lived to even tell the story! We can learn much from history and culture, and in doing so, we do well to retain (where possible) and eat (however possible) the amazing meals that go far *Beyond the Greek Salad*. How did Greece get such a plethora of foods, so diverse in tastes and textures? Every region in Greece has its own unique style and flavor, starting from somewhere and influenced by certain people. Researching, recreating, and bringing these foods to our tables are the provocation for this book and a way to explore what each region specializes in and how we can learn to cook them as daily staples of our repertoire of Greek foods.

Going Beyond the Greek Salad

My curiosity to research the foods of Greece from as early as the fourteenth century onward was a desire of mine for many years, but little did I know what a vast amount of food would appear on my horizon. The deeper I explored, the further I read, the more totally overwhelmed I was at what I found. The superfluous amount of recipes beyond our traditional Greek moussaka, Greek salad, tzatziki, dolmadakia, baklava, or kourambiethes was ever before me. Why have we allowed such richness of food to dissipate from our tables, or have been rarely cooked for starters?

Consequently, my desire was to reproduce, where possible, additional authentic regional foods from around the country, trace back where needed, and find what these dishes were, using the flavors and ingredients to transform them into meals we can easily make in our kitchens of the twenty-first century anywhere in the world. This book combines everything from what the high in society to the peasant people ate at their tables. This book is a compilation of recipes with some adaptations to cooking methods and/or ingredients that may not be as readily available anymore to fit in with our current society, though I have opted to be as authentic as possible.

Social and economic structures made a huge impact on what was eaten. Greece was influenced by surrounding ethnicities. Their modes of cooking were different. Ingredients were taken in their rawest form and cooked as simply and uncomplicatedly as possible, with the avoidance of heavy sauces. What arrayed their tables was vastly different from how we eat today. They had a range of meals pikilia rather than one meal. Meals were important. With food came celebrations, from births to weddings and the like. Food was an important part of gathering people together.

These *paradosiakes sintages* (traditional recipes) were developed and preserved predominantly by the women of the household. In homes of a higher economic status, maids would be the women who prepared all the meals, in contrast with families of medium economic state, wherein the mother-in-law and mothers would do all the cooking. The evening meal was the time when the men would return from work, and the whole family was expected to be seated at the table for the meal. During this time arguments were not to be made, and children had no choice to refuse or select what they would eat. What was placed on their plates was to be eaten.

Each region developed its own local foods with the produce that grew and was cultivated in the designated area. Simple ingredients and aromatic, tasty, and nutritious meals were and are still consumed daily. Nature's wealth, through livestock, herbs, cattle, and sea creatures, are simply what is eaten, even to this day, in Greece.

Meals were made in a selected order. There was a soup followed by a seasonal ladero (an oil-based dish), a main meal of either fish or meat, a salad, and, to end the meal, a compote of stewed or fresh seasonal fruits. Though this sounds abundant, for the low-class people, these dishes were derived from their crops and livestock and therefore did not cost them very much at all. They had *pasta* (cured meats from livestock), *melissokomia* (foods sweetened and enhanced by honey), *tirokomia* (dairy), flour (bread and pies), grape vines (wine and leaves), olives and olive oil, citrus, various crops, *baharika* (the use of various spices), and the abundant ingredient salt.

In this book I highlight regional foods from around Greece that are generally found only in the specified areas. Inexhaustible are the foods of Greece; therefore, I compiled just a few recipes from each region. Over eighty of the most common dishes are in my first book, *Hellenic Kanella: Memories Made in a Greek Kitchen*. This book is not comprehensive by any means, as there are thousands of recipes that can be noted. But one must start somewhere if they are to taste the beauty and history of Greek food, so here is my attempt in over ninety recipes to tempt you to go *Beyond the Greek Salad* to a surfeit of simple yet tasty foods!

Contents

Just Some More	1
Going Beyond the Greek Salad	3
Πρώτο 01: Ionian Islands **Interweaving Charm**	18
Δεύτερο 02: Thessaloniki **The Spice Center**	48
Τρίτο 03: Peloponnese **The Aromatic South**	76
Τέταρτο 04: Epiros **Mountains and Milk**	110
Πέμπτο 05: Crete **Rugged Beauty**	144
Έκτο 06: Aegean Islands **Sea Blue**	164
Έβδομο 07: Thessalía **The Valley**	192
Όγδοο 08: Central Greece **Fusion Foods**	218
Glossary	243
Index	247
Cook's Notes	253
Acknowledgments	254
About the Author	254

Πρώτο 01
Ionian Islands
Νησιά του Ιονίου

19	Σκορδαλιά (Αλιάδα) με μπακαλιάρο **Salt Cod with a Potato-Garlic Dip**
21	Σοφιγάδο - κυδώνι με κρέας **Beef Stew with Quince, Petimezi, and Rosemary**
23	Κερκυραΐικο ψάρι «μπιάνκο» **White Fish with Lemon Emulsion**
25	Σκαρτσοτσέτα **Cheese-Stuffed Veal in Tomato Sauce**
27	Μελιτζάνες σκορδοστούμπι **Baked Eggplants with Garlic Paste**
29	Εργολάβοι (αμυγδαλωτά) με μέλι **Almond and Honey Cookies**
31	Αχλαδάκια **Almond and Orange Little Pears**
33	Παστίτσιο Βενετσιάνικο **Venetian Pastitsio**
37	Πάστα φλώρα με μαρμελάδα σύκο **Pasta Flora with Fig Jam**
39	Κερκυραΐικό Μπουρδέτο, ψάρι με καυτερή σάλτσα **Fish in Spicy Broth**
41	Φριτούρα Ζακύνθου **The Lazy Wife's Bougatsa**
43	Κοτόπουλο κοκκινιστό -ινουμίντο **Chicken "Pollo in umido"**

Δεύτερο 02
Thessaloniki
Θεσσαλονίκη

Κουλούρι Θεσσαλονίκης **Sesame Bread Rings**	49
Ψητά κυδώνια με μπαχαρικά και παγωτό **Baked Quince with Spices and Ice Cream**	51
Μελιτζάνες Ιμάμ μπαϊλντί **Baked Eggplants with Peppers**	53
Μελιτζάνες γλυκό του κουταλιού **Eggplant Spoon Sweet**	55
Καυτερές πιπεριές τουρσί **Pickled Hot Peppers**	57
Μπουγάτσα Θεσσαλονίκης **Custard Pie of Thessaloniki**	59
Μαλεμπί **Muhallebi- Milk Pudding**	61
Μελιτζάνες με γιαούρτι **Eggplant Salad with a Garlic-Lemon Sauce**	63
Χουνκιάρ μπεγερντί **Stewed Aromatic Beef with Eggplant Mash**	65
Παραδοσιακό ραβανί Βέροιας **Revani (Yogurt and Semolina Cake)**	69
Φέτα μπουγιουρντί **Baked Feta Cheese**	72

Τρίτο 03
Peloponnese
Πελοπόννησος

77	Μακαρονόπιτα **Spaghetti and Cheese Pie**
81	Δίπλες **Fried Pastry with Walnuts, Cinnamon, and Honey**
83	Κουλουράκια **Olive Oil and Orange Cookies**
85	Πάστα ελιάς **Tapenade Olive Dip**
87	Κόκορας κρασάτος με χυλοπίτες **Wine-Cooked Rooster with Egg Pasta**
91	Σπανακόρυζο **Spinach Risotto**
93	Μουσταλευριά **Grape Must Pudding**
96	Μουστοκούλουρα **Grape Must and Orange Cookies**
98	Κατσικάκι Φρικασέ με μάραθο και αγκινάρες **Roasted Goat with Dill and Artichokes**
99	Χοιρινό με σέλινο αυγολέμονο **Pork and Celery Stew with an Egg and Lemon Emulsion**
101	Αρακάς λαδερός **Stewed Sweet Peas**
103	Αγκινάρες με αρακά **Braised Artichokes with Baby Peas**
106	Χοιρινό κοκκινιστό με πιπεριές **Pork Stew with Peppers**

Τέταρτο 04
Epiros
Ήπειρος

Γιαννιώτικη Καρυδόπιτα
Chocolate and Walnut Cake — 111

Γαλατόπιτα με χωριάτικο φύλλο
Milk Pie with Homemade Filo Pastry — 113

Φέτα σαγανάκι
Sesame-Coated Feta Saganaki — 117

Γιαννιώτικος μπακλαβάς
Baklava with Shredded Pastry — 121

Ηπειρώτικη Αλευρόπιτα
Yogurt and Cheese Pie — 123

Κεφτεδάκια με γιαούρτι
Spiced Meatballs in a Lemon Yogurt Sauce — 125

Τυρόπιτα με φύλλο κανταΐφι
Cheese Pie with Shredded Pastry — 127

Αρνί κλέφτικο στη λαδόκολλα
Slow-Cooked Lamb and Potatoes in Baking Paper — 129

Λαδόπιτα
Olive Oil Spiced Pie — 130

Πέμπτο 05
Crete
Κρήτη

145   Καλιτσούνια λυχναράκια
Vanilla Pastries

147   Χοχλιοί μπουρμπουριστοί με δεντρολίβανο
Fried Snails with Rosemary

150   Σφακιανές πίτες
Ricotta Pancakes with Honey

151   Ντάκος σαλάτα
Dakos Salad

152   Τσάι από την Κρήτη
Cretan Teas

154   Κοτόπουλο με φασκόμηλο και δεντρολίβανο
Stewed Chicken with Sage and Rosemary

155   Ψητό κοτόπουλο με μανταρίνι, πορτοκαλί, μέλι και θυμάρι
Roast Chicken with Mandarin, Orange, Honey, and Thyme

157   Χόρτα
Wild Weeds with Lemon and Olive Oil

159   Κουλουράκια με μαχλέπι, μαστίχα και πορτοκάλι
Cookies with Mahlepi, Mastiha, and Orange

Έκτο 06
Aegean Islands
Νησιά του Αιγαίου

Ντοματοκεφτέδες Σαντορίνης **Tomato Fritters from Santorini**	165
Κυκλαδική κακαβιά με σαφράν και λευκό κρασί **Fish soup with Saffron and White Wine**	167
Φάβα Σαντορίνης **Split-Pea Puree with Caramelized Onions**	169
Μελόπιτα Σίφνου **Honey Cheesecake from Sifnos**	171
Ρεβύθια φούρνου με δεντρολίβανο (της Καλύμνου) **Baked Chickpeas with Rosemary**	173
Κοτόπουλο με ρεβίθια **Chicken and Chickpea Stew**	175
Κανελάδα (Κως) **Cinnamon Cordial**	177
Μακαρούνες της Κάσου **Yogurt-Coated Pasta with Caramelized Onions and Cheese**	179
Μουούρι Καλύμνου **Shredded Lamb with Currants and Pine Nuts**	181
Χταπόδι στην σκάρα **Grilled Octopus**	182
Μπαρμπούνια τηγανιτά **Pan Fried Red Mullet**	183
Βασιλόπιτα τσουρέκι **New Year's Cake**	185
Σαρδέλες στο φούρνο **Baked Sardines**	187

Έβδομο 07
Thessalia
Θεσσαλία

193	Χαλβάς Φαρσάλων **Caramel Jelly Pudding with Almonds**
195	Κελαϊδή μοσχάρι **Roast Beef with Vegetables and Melted Cheese**
197	Πλαστός **Cornmeal Spinach Pie with No Pastry**
201	Τραχανόσουπα **Soup with Trahana**
203	Τραχανόπιτα χωρίς φύλλο **Trahana Pie with No Pastry**
205	Συκωτάκια με αυγό και λεμόνι **Chicken Livers with Egg and Lemon**
207	Σπετσοφάι με χωριάτικο λουκάνικο **Spicy Stew with Peppers, Sausage, and White Sauce**
209	Σπάτουλα Καλαμπάκας: Καρυδόπιτα με κρέμα **Spiced Walnut Cake with Vanilla Custard Topping**
213	Σουσαμόπιτα **Sesame Pie**

Όγδοο 08
Attiki
Αττική

Πανακότα με μέλι **Greek Yogurt Panacotta with Honey**	219
Κορμός με πορτοκάλι και μέλι **Chocolate Log with Orange and Honey**	221
Τζατζίκι **Tzatziki**	223
Σουβλάκι **Souvlaki**	224
Παντζαροσαλάτα με καρύδια, μήλα, μέλι και γιαούρτι **Beetroot Salad with Walnut, Apple, Honey & Yogurt**	225
Ταχινόπιτα με σοκολάτα, μέλι και ελαιόλαδο **Tahini Cake with Chocolate, Honey & Olive Oil**	227
Χταπόδι τουρσί **Marinated Octopus**	229
Μπιφτέκια με λεμονάτες πατάτες στο φούρνο **Baked Patties with Lemon Potatoes**	231
Ταχινόπιτα μπακλαβά **Spiced Tahini baklava**	233
Κοφτό μακαρονάκι με χταπόδι **Octopus Stew with Pasta**	235
Χτυπητή **Hot Cheese Dip**	237
Φρέντο καπουτσίνο **Freddo Cappuccino**	239
Παγωτό—γιαούρτι η χαλβά **Ice Cream Two Ways—Yoghurt or Halva**	241

Ionian Islands
Πρώτο 01

It is amazing how the history of a place can be embedded in one's taste buds. The Ionian Islands are captured by rich history, including fifty years with the English, and then some influence of the French. Not that one can say they left any prominent flavors on these islands, nor did they themselves embrace, adapt, or replace ingredients such as olive oil or garlic in their own foods (seeing that these were staples on these seven islands). They were passersby regarding food, as were some Turks during the reign of the Ottoman Empire. We see glimpses of their cuisines, but they were not substantially influential. Nevertheless, there is so much to be said about these seven islands and their greater influences.

The land is lush, and the beauty in architecture resembles a mixture of Venetian influences. The islands were part of the Republic of Venice for some four hundred years (from 1386 to 1797). Therefore, to escape the influence of its cuisine would be incomprehensible. Not only were there many Venetians who lived on these islands, but many Venetians came by ship to the main port of Corfu and brought many new products. This was hugely favorable for their economic progress. During this time, the remainder of Greece had come under Ottoman rule, whereas Corfu had become the base for the Venetian fleet, with successive dominations by the Venetians, while also serving as a rescue hub for many Greek scholars and artists escaping the Ottoman territory. The impact and influence in business, in the way food was prepared, and in the language spoken are evident. More than half of the population back in the eighteenth century were Venetian-speaking, as Venice ruled Corfu during the time of the Renaissance. The Italians who lived on the island were called Corfiot-Italians. The reemergence of Greek nationalism was incorporated into Greece in 1864.

So the Venetians were the first to bring to this island products such as corn, tomatoes, green beans, coffee, and chocolate. So with no surprise, then, we see that Corfu more so than the other islands has many best-known dishes from Italian-derived names, such as *pastitsada* (*spezzatino* in Italian), *sofrito*, and *bianco*. While the majority of Greece make use of lemons, in Corfu, still to this day, tomatoes are more readily used—a huge ingredient prominent in Italian cooking. On these islands, we also see the Venetian influence in desserts. The famous *pasta flora* (short-crust pastry), *zabaglione* (cream), *mandolato* (nougat), and *pasteli* (honey nut bar). From seafood and vast specialities, a beautiful robust salami is also made in Lefkada. Kefalonia has many meals made from its known creamy feta, semihard cheese *kefalotyri*, spectacular honey, and the Ionians' finest wine, Robola. Zakinthos, in comparison, accent the Venetian way by their use of garlic. *Skordostoubi* is a garlic dish with which eggplants and/or fish is commonly eaten. We also see the use of particular spices around the *eptanisa* ("seven islands"). *Spetsieriko* is the name given to spices. Paprika and white and black pepper were most commonly used. Cinnamon, nutmeg, and cloves were used by aristocratic families, as they were more expensive until they became more readily available for the everyday household.

Interweaving Charm

Salt Cod with a Potato-Garlic Dip

Σκορδαλιά (Αλιάδα) με μπακαλιάρο

Serves 4 people or 3 cups
1.5 hours
plus overnight soaking
Gluten-Free

Skordalia recipe taken from my other publication: *Hellenic Kanella: Memories Made in a Greek Kitchen*. Skordalia is a silky potato dip with tantalizing lemon and garlic flavor. Skordo means "garlic," and aliada means "puree." This dip is characteristic to the island of Kefalonia. It is made with skill and passion, using a stone mortar and pestle to create the smoothest, silkiest dip. Skordalia from Kefalonia is known as the best in Greece. The main difference between this dip and those of other regions is that Kefalonian skordalia does not use walnuts or bread but rather potatoes and garlic. The texture is smoother and thicker. Pairing fried salted cod with the balance of this garlic-lemon dip is just sublime.

Skordalia:
- 6 medium potatoes (russet), peeled and quartered
- 6 large garlic cloves, minced**
- ½ cup olive oil
- ¾ cup lemon juice
- 1½ teaspoons salt

Place the potatoes in a pot and cover them with water. Boil the potatoes until they are soft.

Drain the potatoes in a colander and add them to a blender.

Add the minced garlic and puree until combined.

Add the olive oil, lemon juice, and salt. Puree again until the dip is mixed well.†

Soak the cod in cold water for a minimum of 15 hours, changing the water at least four times to help remove the salt. Cut into portions and remove any bones. Pat dry on a kitchen towel.

To make the batter, place the beer or soda water, water, yeast, salt, and sugar in a bowl. Whisk to combine and set aside for 10 minutes. Then add the flour and cornstarch, whisking well to remove any lumps. The batter must be of pancake consistency, not too runny or too thick. Set aside, covered with cling film, for a minimum of 30 minutes or until doubled in size.

Take a shallow frying pan and fill with olive oil one-third of the way up. Heat on medium heat. To test if the batter is ready, take a small teaspoon of batter and drop into the pan. If it sizzles immediately, you are now ready for the fish.

Place the extra flour in a bowl and add the fish, coating well and then shaking off any excess flour. Dip the fish into the batter, allowing any excess batter to drip off. Then place into the hot oil. Add 2–3 pieces at a time (do not clutter the pan, as it will cause the temperature to drop drastically, and the fish will soak up too much oil). Fry until golden brown on both sides. Remove and place on a kitchen towel to drain any excess oil. Serve with skordalia and a squeeze of lemon.

Salt Cod:

800 g–1 kg (1.7–2.2 lb. or 28.2–35.2 oz.) salted fresh cod, skin removed‡

350 mL (11.83 fl. oz.) beer or soda water, room temperature

500 mL (16.9 fl. oz.) water

2 teaspoons dried instant yeast

Pinch of salt

Pinch of sugar

1½ cups all-purpose flour*

½ cup corn flour (cornstarch)

1 cup additional flour to coat fish*

Olive oil for frying

*For gluten-free, all-purpose flour can be substituted with cornstarch.
**Mince the garlic in a mortar and pestle with ¼ teaspoon of salt to create a paste.
†Keep the dip refrigerated up to five days.
‡Cod can be substituted with flake or any other white fish.

Beef Stew with Quince, Petimezi, and Rosemary

Σοφιγάδο - κυδώνι με κρέας

Serves 6
1.5 - 2 hours
Gluten-Free

Still retaining its original Italian name and its Venetian gourmet influence on the island, *sofigado* remains a common dish of today. Sofigado is a Mediterranean sweet and sour meal. Quince, the very unpretentious yet somewhat unappealing fruit, is added together with grape must (*petimezi*)* to give a delightfully pleasant taste to this wonderful one-pot dish. Quinces are not overly sweet but slightly tart and work wonderfully well to balance the meatiness of this dish, together with the rosemary adding a beautiful, aromatic savory note. Ensure the quinces are in season!

3/4 cup olive oil, divided

1 kg (2.2 lbs. or 35.2 oz.) beef (blade), cut into bite-size pieces

2 medium onions, diced

2 cups tomato puree

3 sprigs rosemary

5 peppercorns

3 allspice berries (pimento)

Salt and pepper to taste

1 kg (2.2 lbs. or 35.2 oz.) or 3–4 quinces, peeled and quartered

150 mL (5 fl. oz.) grape must/petimezi*

½ cup water

In a large, heavy-based casserole dish (or Dutch oven), heat ½ cup olive oil. Add the meat, browning on both sides. Do this in batches so as to not overcrowd the pot, otherwise they will boil and not brown sufficiently. Place all the browned meat back into the casserole dish, add the onions, and sauté until soft, about 5 minutes. Next add the tomato, rosemary, peppercorns, allspice, salt, and pepper. Ensure the liquid is covering the meat, and if not, add 1 cup (or as much as needed) of water. Allow the meat to simmer on low for 50 minutes or until the meat is three-quarters of the way cooked.

In a separate sauté pan, heat remaining ¼ cup olive oil. Add the quinces and cook for 5 minutes. While they cook, stir together the grape must and ½ cup water. Pour this over the quinces, cover, and cook for a further 5 minutes. Now pour this over the meat mixture (do not stir). Reduce heat, cover, and simmer for an additional 25 minutes or until the meat is falling apart, quinces are soft, and sauce has thickened. Serve with mashed or fried potatoes.

*See description of grape must in glossary. It is available from any Mediterranean grocer.

White Fish with Lemon Emulsion

Κερκυραΐικό ψάρι «μπιάνκο»

Serves 4
35 minutes
Gluten Free

Bianco in Italian means "white," a perfect representation of this dish: white potatoes with white fish, all coated with a lemon and olive oil emulsion. This meal is easy to prepare, makes use of one cooking pan, has very few ingredients, and is very appetizing. Once the potatoes and fish are cooked, they resemble a creamy, poached texture, which melts in the mouth. Lemon and garlic are an intricate part of the cuisine on the Ionian Islands and a very key component to this one-pot dish. Ensure you use boned fish. Some recommendations are flake, John Dory, barramundi, or cod.

6 large potatoes, peeled & sliced into rounds

5 garlic cloves, sliced*

White pepper to taste

Salt to taste

500 g (1.1 lb. or 17.6 oz.) white fish of choice (fillet with no bones)

2 cups water (or as needed)

¾ cup olive oil, divided

2–3 lemons juiced, (to taste)

In a wide pan with a lid, place the potatoes along the bottom of the pan, seasoning well with salt and pepper, then repeat with another layer of potatoes, scattering garlic in between the layers. Place the fish on top of the potatoes, season, then pour in enough water to half-cover the potatoes. The fish will be exposed. Pour half the olive oil into the pan. Cover with the lid and allow it to come to a full boil, then lower the heat and allow to simmer for approximately 20 minutes, or until potatoes are soft, fish is cooked, and liquid has evaporated.

Remove from the heat.

Take the remaining olive oil and lemon juice and place into a jar. Shake well to incorporate, then pour over the fish and potatoes. Swirl the pan around to ensure the emulsion gets distributed throughout the dish. Serve immediately with crusty bread and a glass of white wine.

*Tip: If you don't prefer a strong garlic taste, you can cut the clove in half and remove the membrane. This is the part that gives garlic its intense aroma.

Cheese-Stuffed Veal in Tomato Sauce

Σκαρτσοτσέτα

Serves 4
1–5 hours

Who would have thought a one-pot wonder of veal, tomatoes, and Greek cheeses would be so wonderful? First thought as you look at it is the resemblance to the known *involtini*, the classically known Italian word derived from involto, basically meaning a "bundle" or "wrap." Others say the word *skartsotsetta* is derived from the Italian word (*scartocetti*) for pockets. On the island, skartsotsetta parcels can be either pastry pockets filled with veal or veal filled with cheeses, such as the recipe below. These parcels on the island of Zakinthos no doubt have become an adaptation or reworking of the original dish, influenced by the Italians. The veal wraps are cooked in a simmering salsa and stuffed with Greek cheeses. This is a great main meal to share with the accompaniment of roasted potatoes and a side salad.

700 g (1.5 lb. or 24.69 oz.) veal or beef cutlets

½ cup crushed roasted almonds to serve (optional)

Filling:
¾ cup flat-leaf parsley, chopped

2 garlic cloves, minced

Salt and pepper to taste

½ cup bread crumbs

2 hard boiled eggs, cut into small pieces (optional)

½ cup feta cheese, crumbled

½ cup kefalograviera cheese*, grated

1/3 cup olive oil

Sauce:
½ cup olive oil

1 cup white wine

2 cups tomato puree

1 bay leaf

Salt and pepper to taste

1 tablespoon castor (superfine) sugar

Prepare the veal by pounding it as thinly as possible. Set aside.

Place all the ingredients for the filling in a bowl and mix well to combine. Take one veal cutlet and season with some salt and pepper. Spread two tablespoons of the filling mixture and gently roll up, enclosing it with a toothpick. Do the same with all the remaining veal.

To make the sauce. Take a wide sauté pan with a lid and heat the olive oil. Place the veal rolls into the pan, browning well on both sides. Now add the wine and allow it to cook for 3 minutes. Pour over the tomato puree, bay leaf, salt and pepper, and sugar. Allow to cook on a medium heat, covered, ensuring there is enough liquid to cover the veal rolls halfway up. If not, add 1–2 cups boiled water. Cook for 30–45 minutes or until veal is totally cooked. Remove lid and cook for a further 10 minutes until the sauce has thickened slightly and oil has surfaced to the top. Serve immediately with scattered almonds over the top.

*See description of Kefalograviera cheese in glossary. Can be substituted with Parmesan cheese. Available at Mediterranean grocers.

Baked Eggplants with Garlic Paste

Μελιτζάνες σκορδοστούμπι

Serves 4-5
1 hour
Gluten-Free

Skordostoubi means "stuffed with garlic" and is a name also given to fish or other vegetables that have this garlic sauce added. The mixture of garlic and vinegar is added to a honey and tomato base sauce that gets poured over the fried eggplants. Adding vinegar is key to balancing the garlic and honey. Though more commonly used for marinating meat, the vinegar in this case really enhances the flavor and brings out a rich, savory note unique to this dish. Most commonly eaten in Zakynthos, skordostoubi has been documented to have come about from Venetian influence.

6 garlic cloves, minced

4 teaspoons red wine vinegar

1 cup olive oil, divided

2 cups tomato puree

1 tablespoon honey

Black pepper (to taste)

Salt to taste

2 plump eggplants, sliced into 1-cm (0.4-in.) rounds

1½ cups kasseri cheese*, grated (optional)

Yogurt to serve

*See description of Kasseri cheese in glossary. It is available from Mediterranean delicatessens. Romano or Parmesan cheese can be substituted.

Preheat oven to 220°C (428°F).

In a small bowl, combine garlic and vinegar. Set aside. In a small saucepan, heat 4 tablespoons of olive oil. Add the tomato puree, honey, pepper, and salt, then the garlic and vinegar mix. Cook on medium heat until the sauce has thickened slightly (10–15 minutes).

Fry the eggplants in batches, using a few tablespoons of olive oil at a time and adding more oil when needed. Don't be shy on the olive oil—it adds beautiful flavor. Season and set aside.

To assemble, take a baking dish (20 cm x 28 cm or 7.8 in. x 11 in.) and layer one row of eggplants. To this add around four soup spoons of sauce over the eggplants. Sprinkle some cheese on top. Repeat with a second layer (you may have a little leftover sauce; just discard it). Top with the cheese and bake for 30 minutes or until golden and the oil has surfaced to the top.

Serve warm with crusty bread or dolloped with yogurt.

Tip: Feel free to add more garlic! This dish can be assembled into the baking tray a few hours ahead and baked 40 minutes before intended to be eaten.

Almond and Honey Cookies

Εργολάβοι (Αμυγδαλωτά) με μέλι

Serves 20 pieces
35 minutes
Gluten-Free

Amigdalo is the word for "almond." Very commonly known as happiness or new beginning cookies, these are baked on celebratory occasions. The biscuits are the equivalent of a macaroon, crispy on the outside and chewy on the inside. It is slightly sweetened with the addition of honey and highlights the great texture and taste of almonds. The egg whites in this recipe with the technique of hot honey create a slightly denser cookie than that of the next recipe *Almond and orange little pears*.

- 200 g (0.44 lb. or 7.05 oz.) almond meal
- 100 g (0.22 lb. or 3.5 oz.) castor (superfine) sugar
- 1 teaspoon lemon zest (optional)
- Pinch of salt
- 2 medium eggs, whites only, approximately 70 g (0.15 lb. or 2.46 oz.)
- 20 g (0.04 lb. or 0.7 oz.) runny honey
- 3 tablespoons amaretto liquor or almond extract
- 100 g (0.22 lb. or 3.5 oz.) flaked almonds
- 1½ cups icing (confectioners) sugar (optional)

Place the almond meal, castor sugar, lemon zest, and salt in a bowl. Mix to combine and set aside.

Using an electric mixer, beat the egg whites on high until soft peaks have formed. In the meantime, heat the honey in a saucepan and allow it to boil for around 20 seconds. Remove from heat and slowly pour the honey along the inside of the mixer, whisking until the meringue is fully whipped and the bowl of the mixer has cooled (place hands under the bowl to feel if the honey has cooled). Add the almond extract and mix to incorporate. Remove the bowl from the mixer and slowly add spoonfuls of the almond mixture, incorporating well with a wooden spoon. Place the mixture into a clean bowl covered with plastic wrap and refrigerate for 30–40 minutes to firm up.

Line a baking tray with baking paper. Preheat oven to 160°C (350°F). Take two bowls. In one, place the flaked almonds, and in the other, place the icing sugar.

Remove the almond mixture from the fridge. Gently take small spoonfuls, around 30 g (0.06 lb. or 1.05 oz.) each, and roll into balls. Gently toss into the flaked almonds and press to ensure they stick. Then gently toss into the icing sugar to coat (this is optional, if you want them to have a white snow effect once baked). Place onto baking tray, pressing down slightly to flatten. Bake for 15–20 minutes or until golden but still soft. Keep an eye on them, as they can burn very quickly. Allow to cool on a rack. To store, place in a sealed container for up to one week.

Almond and Orange Little Pears

Αχλαδάκια

Serves 20 pieces
35 minutes
Gluten-Free, Dairy-Free, Egg-Free

When a sweet treat is dairy-free, egg-free, gluten-free, and unbaked, it can be shared at any event. These are incredibly quick to make and can be stored up to three months. They get their name, which is "small pears" in Greek, from their shape. You can make them into round balls, but the pear shape just looks delicately sophisticated and pretty. The main ingredient is almonds, and then depending on what flavor profile one desires, they can be adapted. The list of flavors is endless. In the Ionian Islands, flavor choices vary among honey, orange, koniak or Amaretto, cinnamon, and mandarin as some of the choices.

250 g (0.55 lb. or 8.81 oz.) almond meal

100 g (0.22 lb. or 3.5 oz.) icing (confectioners) sugar

1½ oranges, zested

50 mL (1.69 fl. oz.) orange juice or liquor

1 cup icing (confectioners) sugar, plus additional for outer coating

20 whole cloves

In a bowl, place the almond meal, 100 g of sugar, and zest. Mix to combine well. Add three-quarters of the liquid to begin with, then mix with your hands to combine. The mixture is ready once you can roll small ball shapes in your hand that hold their shape. If the mixture is not pliable or is too sticky, add a little more almond meal; if it is too dry, add a little more liquid until you can shape them. Do not overmix.

In another bowl, add the extra 1 cup icing sugar. Measure out 25 g (0.05 lb. or 0.88 oz.) balls. Shape into a pear, then place into the icing sugar, coating well. Add a clove on top.

Store in an airtight container for up to two months. These are best served with a cup of strong coffee.

Tip: For mastiha-flavored pears, add mastiha liquor (instead of orange) and 1 drop mastiha essence or 1 mastiha resin (crushed). Mastiha is the resin from the mastic tree and forms in small crystalline drops. See description in glossary for more.

Venetian Pastitsio

Παστίτσιο Βενετσιάνικο

Serves 8-10
2.5 hours

Most people are aware of the well-known Greek dish *pastitsio* (from *pasticcio*, meaning "pasta pie," in Italian). It was first invented in the early twentieth century by Chef Nikolaos Tselementes. He was a French-trained Greek chef who authored Greece's most widespread cookbook, *Greek Cookery,* first published in 1910. Chef Nikolaos was known for adjusting traditional recipes with his French training and detesting certain spices, as they reminded him of the Ottoman rule. So from the original Italian-style *pasticcio*, he reinvented it by removing the pastry, adding butter rather than oil, and adding milk and flour, and thus, he made the traditional Greek pastitsio we know of today, served throughout Greece at every *taverna* and in the common household. Furthermore, the *Venetian Pastitsio* (commonly served in Corfu) has the good of both worlds—it has a semisweet pastry case (which comes together very easily) and a beautiful mix of spiced bolognaise and fried bacon, all huddled together with cheese. It is a great meal to serve a crowd and, yes, a little more indulgent. It is traditionally baked in a high cake tin, but a shorter tin will do just fine. The meat sauce can be made a day ahead and just reheated when assembling the dish to speed up the process.

Meat sauce:
½ cup olive oil

3 garlic cloves, minced

500 g (1.1 lb. or 17.6 oz.) minced beef

1½ teaspoons salt

1 teaspoon black pepper

2 teaspoons cinnamon powder

6 whole cloves

½ teaspoon ground cloves

1 cinnamon quill

1 bay leaf

2 tablespoons tomato paste

2 cups tomato puree

1 cup red wine

1½ cups water

2 teaspoons castor (superfine) sugar

Start by making the meat sauce. Heat the oil in a medium pan over medium heat. Add the garlic and sauté until it starts to sizzle, being careful not to burn it. Add the beef to the pan. Season with salt and pepper. Using a wooden spoon, start to break up the meat, allowing it to brown well. Do not hurry this step—it is crucial to take it slowly. Brown the meats until all the juices have evaporated and the oil has come to the surface. Add the cinnamon powder, cloves, cinnamon quill, and bay leaf, and cook for 1 minute. Add the tomato paste and cook for another 3 minutes. Add the tomato puree, wine, 1½ cups water, and sugar. Simmer the sauce over low heat, covered, until the meat is cooked, the sauce has reduced, and oil has come to the surface. This takes approximately 35–40 minutes. Set the sauce aside.

To make the pastry: In a bowl, whisk the oil and sugar so that it comes together. Add the eggs, orange juice, and zest and whisk to combine. Using a wooden spoon, slowly incorporate the flour to form a dough that is soft but does not stick to your hands. Add more flour if necessary. Roll out onto a board and knead. Roll into a ball and allow the dough to rest, covered with a clean towel.

Fry the bacon in some olive oil until golden. Remove from pan, draining any excess oil. Set aside.

Cook spaghetti as per packet ingredients, ensuring noodles are not overcooked, as they will also cook in the oven. Rinse, then place in a big bowl together with the meat sauce, 2 cups of cheese, and beaten eggs. Mix well to combine. Set aside.

Preheat oven to 200°C (392°F).

Grease a springform tin 25 cm (9.8 in.) in diameter with olive oil. Take three-quarters of the dough and, using a rolling pin, roll out into a large pizza base large enough to cover the base of the tin and up the sides. Place the pastry into the tin, carefully pressing down and along the sides to create a pie case. Take half of the bacon and sprinkle along the bottom. Pour in the spaghetti and meat mixture, pressing down to fill in any gaps. Top with the remaining bacon and remaining cheese. Now take the pastry that is remaining and roll out a sheet large enough to cover the top. Push down with your hands to cover, joining the ends all the way around to seal the pie. Cover and bake at 160°C (320°F) for 1 hour 30 minutes or until golden. Allow to completely cool, then flip (so that the bottom is on the top) onto a large serving platter (remove the cake tin) and slice into wedges. Serve with extra cheese and a salad. The dish keeps in the refrigerator, covered with cling film, for up to three days. It tastes even better the next day.

*See description of Kefalotyri cheese in glossary. It can be substituted with Parmesan cheese.

Semisweet dough:
150 mL (5 fl. oz.) olive oil

50 g (0.11 lb. or 1.7 oz.) castor (superfine) sugar

2 whole eggs

¾ cup orange juice, freshly squeezed

½ an orange, zested

450 g (0.99 lb. or 15.8 oz.) all-purpose flour

1 cup bacon, chopped into small cubes

250 g (0.55 lb. or 8.81 oz.) spaghetti or tubular pasta (#5 if using a Greek brand)

2½ cups grated kefalotyri cheese*, divided

2 whole eggs, beaten

Venetian Pastitsio, page 33

Pasta Flora with Fig Jam

Πάστα φλώρα με μαρμελάδα σύκο

Serves 8
1.5 hours

In Greece, this dessert is called *pasta flora*, or otherwise known as *pasta frola*, derived from the Italian word for "short-crust pastry." Some say the origins come from Argentina, others Uruguay or Italy, and others Greece. Whatever the case, it has similarities to various recipes but primarily the Italian recipe for *crostata* (another variation of a filled tart). Pasta flora is a common dessert and breakfast snack to have with coffee throughout Greece. The abundance of figs in Greece means that fresh, homemade fig jam is always on hand to add to this delicious short-crust pastry. Commonly, tarts require "blind baking" (a process of cooking the tart shell with rice or beans until partially golden) and are then filled. Pasta flora, though, differs in that the filling is added prior to any baking, and the pastry is made with olive oil (my choice for a lighter version). I characteristically prefer a light olive oil for this recipe due to its mild flavor, which pairs wonderfully well with the sweet jam. This makes a very quick and easy dessert.

300 g (0.66 lb. or 10.5 oz.) all-purpose flour

110 g (0.24 lb. or 3.88 oz.) almond meal

150 g (0.33 lb. or 5.29 oz.) icing (confectioners) sugar, sieved

1 whole egg, plus 1 yolk

Pinch of salt

1 teaspoon baking powder

115 mL (3.89 fl. oz.) light olive oil

3 tablespoons cold water

1½ cups fig jam*

Icing (confectioners) sugar, to serve

In a food processor, place the flour, almond meal, icing sugar, eggs, salt, and baking powder. Pulse together until it resembles fine bread crumbs. Add the oil and one teaspoon of water at a time. Pulse until the dough comes together, adding one more tablespoon of water if required. Tip onto a work surface and use your hands to gently press the dough into a disc. Wrap in cling film and allow to rest in the fridge for 20 minutes.

Preheat oven to 160°C (320°F).

Remove from the fridge, separating one-quarter of the dough. Place this quarter back in the fridge. Roll the remaining dough between two pieces of parchment paper a little larger than the tart case and ½ cm (1.9 in.) in thickness. You don't want a thick crust! Gently place the dough in a tart case 35 cm x 12 cm (13.77 in. x 4.72 in.), pressing down and up the sides. Spoon jam on top, making sure it is evenly distributed. Take the remaining pastry out of the fridge and roll between the parchment paper. With a pastry cutter or a knife, cut out long strips and create a lattice or desired pattern, then place over the jam. Bake for 40 minutes or until golden at 160°C (320°F). Allow to cool before removing the mold. Serve at room temperature with a sprinkling of icing sugar or cold the following day. Keep for up to one week, covered, in the refrigerator.

*Any jam of choice can be used.

Fish in Spicy Broth

Κερκυραΐικο Μπουρδέτο, ψάρι με καυτερή σάλτσα

Serves 4
1 hour
Gluten-Free

This dish represents the island of Corfu on a plate! *Bourdeto* is the Venetian word for "broth" and a specialty dish from this island. It is fish simmered in a rich, spicy broth. Red spicy paprika are added to onions, garlic, and olive oil, and then fish is added and simmered gently. Whole scorpion fish is preferable, but fillets will work as well. The vibrant red color is achieved by the hot and sweet paprika. Optimum flavor is achieved when all the liquid has evaporated and the olive oil has surfaced to the top. Grab some bread to dip into this sauce and enjoy with a glass of wine. This dish has few ingredients yet is packed with flavor! Freshly ground paprika is key, as this is where the flavor comes from!

1 cup olive oil

3 large onions, diced

1 garlic clove, minced

4 tablespoons sweet paprika

1 tablespoon hot paprika (optional)

Salt and pepper to taste

2 tablespoons castor (superfine) sugar

700 g (1.54 lb. or 24.69 oz.) white fish (e.g., rockling, flake), cleaned, gutted, and portioned

1–2 cups boiled water

In a wide saucepan and on medium heat, add oil and onions, sautéing until soft. Add garlic, sweet and hot paprika, salt, pepper, and sugar. Mix through, then add the fish. Add one cup boiled water (or a little more) to just cover the fish. Place a lid on the saucepan and allow to simmer on low for 30–40 minutes.

Remove lid, taste for seasoning, and adjust if needed. Allow it to cook uncovered for another 20 minutes or until the juices have evaporated and the oil has surfaced to the top. Serve with crusty bread or rice.

The Lazy Wife's Bougatsa

Φριτούρα Ζακύνθου

Serves 16 pieces
15 minutes plus 10 hours refrigeration

This is an authentic dessert from the island of Zakynthos. It is a poor man's food, made with very few ingredients. It has a crispy exterior with a soft center, which tastes like the famous Thessaloniki's *bougatsa*. It is easy to make (a cheat's version if you love bougatsa) and can be half-prepared in advance and kept covered in the refrigerator. Once you are ready for dessert, a quick light fry in the pan and a sprinkle of cinnamon and sugar is all you need. This is best eaten hot.

750 mL (25.36 fl. oz.) water

Pinch of salt

250 g (0.55 lb. or 8.81 oz.) fine semolina flour

Olive oil to shallow fry

Cinnamon to serve

Castor (superfine) sugar to serve

Place the water and salt in a saucepan and bring to a boil. Slowly pour in the semolina, stirring with a wooden spoon continuously so that no lumps form. Cook on medium heat until a thick consistency has been achieved and water has totally evaporated. This will take a few minutes. Remove from heat and pour into lightly oiled baking tray 20 cm (7.87 in.) square. Flatten to have an even layer. Allow to cool completely, then cover with cling film and place in refrigerator for 10 hours or overnight.

Slice pieces (as desired). Heat 3–4 tablespoons oil in a pan. Place the semolina squares (as many as can fit into your pan) into the hot oil and allow to cook on medium heat, turning once to ensure a golden, crisp exterior has been achieved. Immediately sprinkle cinnamon and sugar to coat both sides. Serve immediately.

Tip: You can add more oil and deep-fry the semolina squares. This way you will get an even crispier exterior.

Chicken "Pollo in umido"

Κοτόπουλο κοκκινιστό -ινουμίντο

Serves 5
1 hour

In Corfu this dish is called in umido (ινουμιντο), meaning "stew" in Italian. It is not a recipe, per se, but rather a method of cooking. This dish is completely cooked in its own juices, together with wine and tomato. It is not exclusive to poultry; the same recipe can be used for seafood and red meat. To acquire the best result, the cooking should be done on a low heat with a heavy lid, to ensure the steam remains in the pot as it cooks. A delicious, thick sauce is obtained, which pairs wonderfully with rice, mashed potatoes, or spaghetti.

1 whole chicken, cut into pieces

1 cup all-purpose flour for dusting

½ cup olive oil

4 cups white wine

2 tablespoons tomato paste

250 g (0.55 lb. or 8.81 oz.) tomato puree

1 tablespoon rosemary, chopped

2 bay leaves

2 cinnamon quills

2 allspice berries (pimento)

Pepper and salt to taste

1 tablespoon castor (superfine) sugar

In a bowl, place the chicken and flour and season with salt and pepper. Mix to combine and set aside.

In a heavy-based pan, heat the oil. Shake off excess flour from the chicken and brown well on all sides. Once browned, place in a bowl. Add the wine to the pan, scraping off any bits that have stuck to the bottom of the pan with a wooden spoon. Allow to cook for 3 minutes, then add tomato paste, tomato puree, rosemary, bay leaves, cinnamon, allspice, salt, pepper, and sugar and mix to combine. Allow to come to a boil, then return chicken pieces to the pan. Make sure the chicken is covered with juices. If not, add some more wine or water (½–1 cup).

Cook on a low heat, covered, for 40 minutes or until the chicken is cooked through and the sauce has reduced by half and thickened. Serve hot with potato mash.

Thessaloniki
Δεύτερο 02

Thessaloniki, the city opulent in antiquity and known for outstanding food, was named after the royal daughter of Kassandros in 316 BC. The name would be incessantly embedded in honor of her, commemorating a military victory. Here, we have the greatest military leader the world has ever known, Alexander the Great! Alexander founded close to seventy cities around the Mediterranean, spreading the Greek culture and trade. He ensured that the Greeks remained dominant, inspiring and bringing to life the profound Hellenistic period! Alexander the Great drank wines from this region that are still produced to this day. Byzantine flavors and the coexistence of Turkish, Greek, French, and Jewish communities meant superfluity in an absolute melting pot of many cuisines, and influences in the style of cooking and dishes were created and still exist! This is the city that captures crossroads of flavors from surrounding countries, the gastronomic capital that enhances taste buds with flavors!

This region is very much like a bountiful garden. From fields laden with saffron crocus to vast orchard trees with ample cherries, apricots, and apples, to its flaming red and sweet Florina peppers. Many dishes were brought in from Pontus and refugees from Smyrna (now Izmir), who fled in 1922. Not much else, other than the clothes on their backs and their cuisine embedded in their hearts, was brought into Greece. With them came Greeks from Constantinople, who added much spice to the cuisine with the usage of cinnamon and clove, along with an overabundance of syrup-drenched desserts spiced with the influence of Turkey and beyond. Meat dishes combined with fruits were common, such as quinces, chestnuts with meat, chicken with apricots and almonds, or meatballs with prunes. But two main staples known throughout Thessaloniki are no doubt *bougatsa* (the custard-, cheese-, or meat-filled pastry) and the street snack *koulouri*. These bread rings are distinctively flavorsome because of the high-quality sesame seeds that are used to coat the bread rings. One cannot omit the fact that drinking coffee was also a very popular routine of the day. Back in the day, men predominantly would drink up to thirty (very small) cups of coffee while smoking pipes. Many aromatic herbs were used both in foods and on the body for medicinal purposes.

Thessaloniki is the city that has historical landmarks with beautiful charm, along with colorful and chaotic culinary influences that have given us a cuisine of blended flavors to invigorate our senses. We get hot and spicy, fresh and mild, and complex all at the same time.

Sesame Bread Rings

Κουλούρι Θεσσαλονίκης

Serves 10 pieces
1 hour 40 minutes

The renowned street food of Thessaloniki is the *koulouri*. They say the birthplace of this bread was Thessaloniki via Greek refugees from Asia Minor. Food street vendors during the Byzantine Empire sold these breads in Constantinople, and to this day, a version is made in Turkey called *simi*. Street vendors at every corner have an array of these piled up high, freshly baked in mobile glass displays or large rustic baskets. They have a chewy center and nutty exterior and are somewhat slightly sweetened from the dunking in petimezi (grape must syrup) before sesame gets enclosed around them. They can be eaten as they are or with some cheese. *Koulouri* means "a round-shaped bread ring."

225 mL (7.6 fl. oz.) lukewarm water, divided

3 teaspoons dried instant yeast

1½ tablespoons castor (superfine) sugar

2 tablespoons olive oil

100 mL (3.38 fl. oz.) whole milk, lukewarm

1 whole egg

1½ teaspoons salt

Approximately 630–650 g (1.38–1.43 lb. or 22.2 oz.) all-purpose flour

1/3 cup grape must syrup (petimezi)*, diluted in ¼ cup water

2½ cups sesame seeds, toasted

*Petimezi/grape must is available at Middle Eastern or Mediterranean delicatessens.

Attach a dough hook to a stand mixer. In the bowl of the mixer, add ¼ cup water, yeast, and sugar. Mix with a wooden spoon to dilute. To this, immediately add the remaining water, oil, milk, egg, and salt and slowly add the flour (reserve the last 20 g, or 0.04 lb., in case the flour mixture does not need it). On medium speed, mix for approximately 5 minutes or until the mixture comes away from the bowl. It will be slightly sticky but also soft. Add a little more flour if it is too sticky and difficult to handle. Remove and knead for 2 minutes on a work surface and form into a ball. Place 2 tablespoons of olive oil in the mixing bowl and place kneaded dough. Cover and allow to rise for approximately 40 minutes.

In the meantime, place the grape must into another bowl with the water. Mix and set aside. In another bowl, place the toasted sesame. Once the dough has risen, remove from the bowl and divide into 10 pieces (100 g, or 0.22 lb., each). Do not flour your workbench, as you want the dough to stick slightly. Knead each piece slightly to deflate any air. Roll each piece into a rope approximately 45 cm (17.7 in.) long. Bring the ends together into a ring shape and press to seal. Wash and wipe hands after each koulouri, as the sesame mixture sticks to your hands.

Line two baking trays with parchment paper. Preheat oven to 200°C (392°F).

Dip each ring into the grape must, then immediately into the sesame. Coat well and place onto the baking tray. Bake for 20 minutes. These can be eaten warm or cold.

Baked Quince with Spices and Ice Cream

Serves 6
1.5 hours
Gluter-Free

Ψητά κυδώνια με μπαχαρικά και παγωτό

Quince fruit, together with apples and pears, belongs to the *Cydonia oblonga* family. They originated in the Caucasian area, then spread to the Mediterranean and the East. Formerly, in the Greek language, the fruit was known as *strouthia*. The name was changed as the fruit started to also grow in abundance on the island of Crete in the region of Cydonia (*Kidonia*), hence, the Greek name *kidoni*. Due to their very high amount of pectin (a natural thickener), quinces are commonly made into jams and compotes. The thickening agent in them makes them perfect for making preserves without any added pectin. Once cooked, quince takes on a beautiful pink color, has a mild sweetness, and releases a lovely perfume. They pair wonderfully well with spices and are mouthwatering with yogurt or ice cream.

3 large quinces, washed, skins on

1 lemon, juiced

½ cup brown (*muscovado*) sugar

8 whole cloves

2 cinnamon quills

¼ cup mastiha or ouzo liquor (optional)*

½ a vanilla bean, split and with seeds removed

2 star anise

2 tablespoons cinnamon powder to serve

Vanilla ice cream (or Greek yogurt) to serve

Crushed pistachios to serve

Cinammon powder to serve

Preheat oven to 180°C (356°F).

Wash and halve the quinces, scooping out the core with a paring knife (or quarter them if the core is very hard to remove).** Place in a deep baking dish just large enough to fit all the quinces. Do not use a huge dish with big gaps. Brush the quinces with lemon juice.

Quarter-fill the baking dish with water. Sprinkle the sugar over the quinces. Add the cloves, cinnamon, liquor, vanilla bean, and star anise. Cover baking tray with a lid or foil. Bake for 1 hour or until the quinces are soft but still retain their shape. Remove from oven. Allow to cool (preferably), although they can be served warm. Serve with vanilla ice cream, scattered pistachios, a drizzle of syrup from the baking dish, and a sprinkle of cinnamon powder.

*Mastiha or ouzo liquor can be purchased from any Mediterranean deli or liquor store.

**Tip: Boil the cores with 1 cup water for 5–6 minutes. Strain and add this water to the dish with the quinces. The cores have pectin, which releases, making the end liquid slightly gelatinous once cooked.

Baked Eggplants with Peppers

Μελιτζάνες Ιμάμ μπαϊλντί

Serves 4-6
1 hour 20 minutes
Gluten-Free

By the name of this dish, there is no guessing that it has originated from Turkey. *Imam Baildi* means "the priest fainted." This dish made its way to Greece through the Ottoman Empire. Story has it that an imam fainted when his wife served him this dish because of sheer delight at its taste. Others say that he fainted in horror upon hearing how much olive oil went into the dish. I would suggest both could be true, and yet it is still well worth cooking. It is a dish that is extremely tasty, enhanced, no doubt, by the amount of olive oil.

Olive oil for frying

5 thin eggplants (otherwise known as Japanese eggplants)

¾ cup olive oil

2 onions, sliced thinly

2 spring onions, finely chopped

1 green capsicum, chopped

2 garlic cloves, minced

¼ cup flat-leaf parsley, chopped

¾ cup red or white wine

2 tablespoons tomato paste

¾ cup tomato puree

2 teaspoons castor (superfine) sugar

1 cup water

Salt and pepper to taste

1 bay leaf

3 sprigs thyme

¼ cup kasseri cheese*, grated

¾ cup feta cheese, crumbled

Slice eggplants in half lengthwise. Cover the base of the frying pan with olive oil. Allow to heat up on medium heat. Place eggplants flesh side down into the hot oil. Fry on medium heat until slightly golden. Turn over and repeat on the skin side. Once the eggplants are soft and colored, remove and set aside on a kitchen paper towel. Sprinkle with salt.

In another pan, sauté the onions in the ¾ cup of olive oil. Cook on medium heat for 10 minutes or until very soft. Add spring onions, capsicum, garlic, parsley, and wine and cook for a further 5 minutes. To this add paste, tomato puree, sugar, water, bay leaf, and thyme and season liberally. Allow to cook half-covered on medium-to-low heat for 15–20 minutes or until the sauce has thickened slightly.

Preheat oven to 200°C (392°F). Take one-quarter of the mixture and place in the bottom of the baking dish. Place eggplants on top, skin side down. With a fork, gently press down onto the flesh to allow the onion mixture to sit in the eggplant. Spoon the remaining onion mixture into and over the eggplants, being very generous. Bake for 20 minutes or until golden, ensuring that the oil has surfaced to the top and the liquid has evaporated. Serve with crumbled feta or grated kasseri cheese. This dish can be eaten hot or at room temperature.

*Kasseri cheese can be purchased from Mediterranean grocers. It can be substituted with grated Parmesan cheese.

Eggplant Spoon Sweet

Serves 25 pieces
2-3 hours
plus 27 hours overnight soaking
Gluten-Free

Μελιτζάνες γλυκό του κουταλιού

Spoon sweets are known to have originated in Greece around the fourteenth century, when Arab traders brought sugar to their shores. Sugar evidently became more available and economically viable, and with the consumption of fruits came the spoon sweet. I have used a little more sugar than usual to achieve a semiburnt-like caramel to the syrup. Spoon sweets are served with a glass of cold water, and no more than one teaspoon is ever served at any one time. This is a sweet that is gluten-free and has no animal fats.

25 baby eggplants (as small as you can get, otherwise they will have too many seeds)

2 lemons, juiced, plus the skins

700 mL (23.6 fl. oz.) water

500 g (1.1 lb. or 17.6 oz.) castor (superfine) sugar

8 whole cloves

½ teaspoon vanilla sugar

Half-fill a bowl with water, adding the juice of 1½ lemons. Do not discard the skins. Set aside.

With a potato peeler or a sharp paring knife, peel the eggplants and cut off the stem. Rub each cleaned eggplant with juiced lemon skins, then place into the lemon-water bowl. Once they have all been peeled, place a plate on top to weigh down the eggplants. Allow to stand for 20 hours (this helps release any bitterness from the eggplants).

After 20 hours, drain the eggplants. Set aside. Place a pot on the stove with the 700 mL (23.6 fl. oz.) of water, sugar, cloves, and vanilla. On a low heat, allow the sugar to dissolve (around 10 minutes). Immediately place the eggplants and the remaining juice of half the lemon. Allow to cook for around 2–3 hours. They are ready when there is no bitterness when tasting the eggplant. Remove the eggplants and place into a sterilized jar. Keep cooking the syrup until it has reduced and is at a glucose consistency. Pour syrup over the eggplants, covering them completely. Keep for 1–2 months in a dry, cool place.

Pickled Hot Peppers

Καυτερές πιπεριές τουρσί

Serves 2 jars
20 minutes
plus 3 weeks to pickle
Gluten-Free

Pickling is an old tradition for Greeks, going back to when household refrigeration did not exist. The brine is made with wine vinegar, salt, and olive oil, key staples that Greeks always had and have on hand. Pickling was and is the way of sustaining produce throughout the year and preserving perishable foods for months on end. The Greek word used is *toursi*.

200 g (0.44 lb. or 7.05 oz.) small hot peppers

3 whole garlic cloves

1 tablespoon peppercorns

2 bay leaves

1 tablespoon coarse salt

2 cups white wine vinegar

½ cup olive oil

Wash and score the peppers two to three times. Divide the peppers between two small or place in one large sterilized jar(s). Place the peppers in the jar(s) tightly, adding the garlic, peppercorns, bay leaves, and salt. Pour in enough vinegar to just cover the peppers. Now add olive oil to fully cover everything in the jar. If the oil is not covering everything, the peppers will mold. Seal and place in a cupboard away from direct sunlight for three weeks to pickle. They can then be consumed. Store at room temperature.

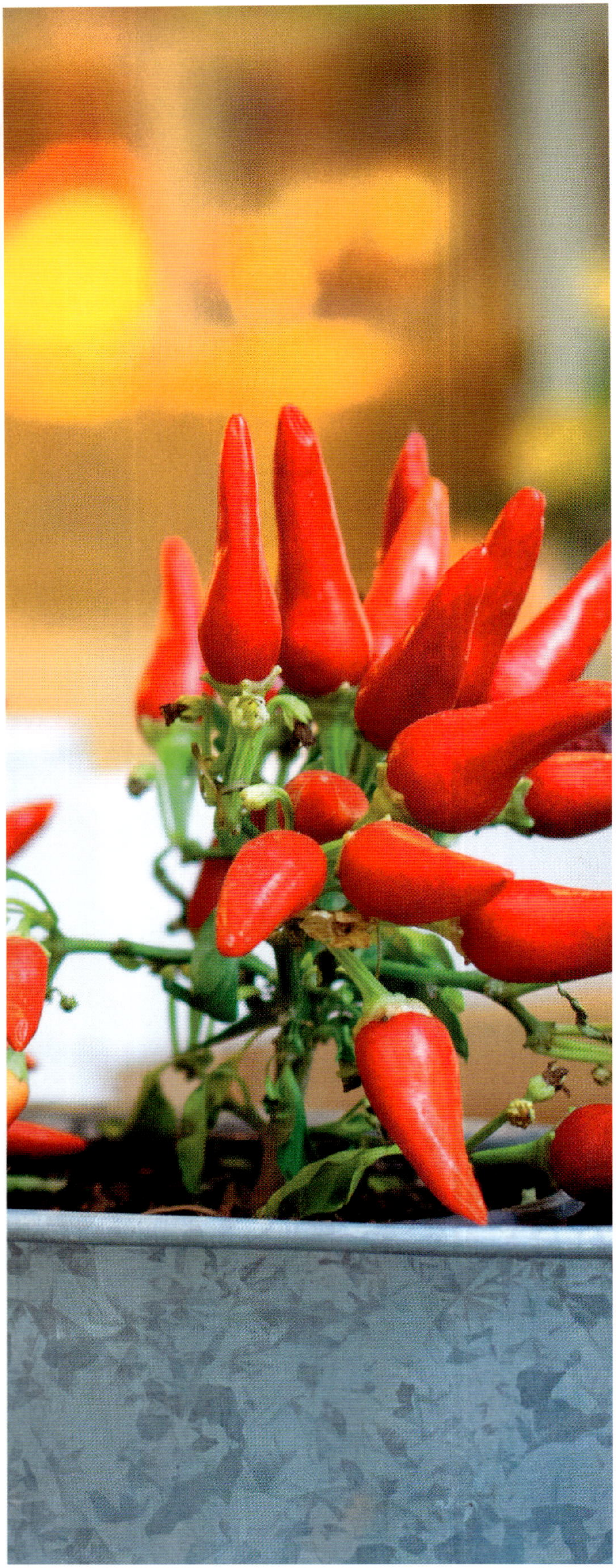
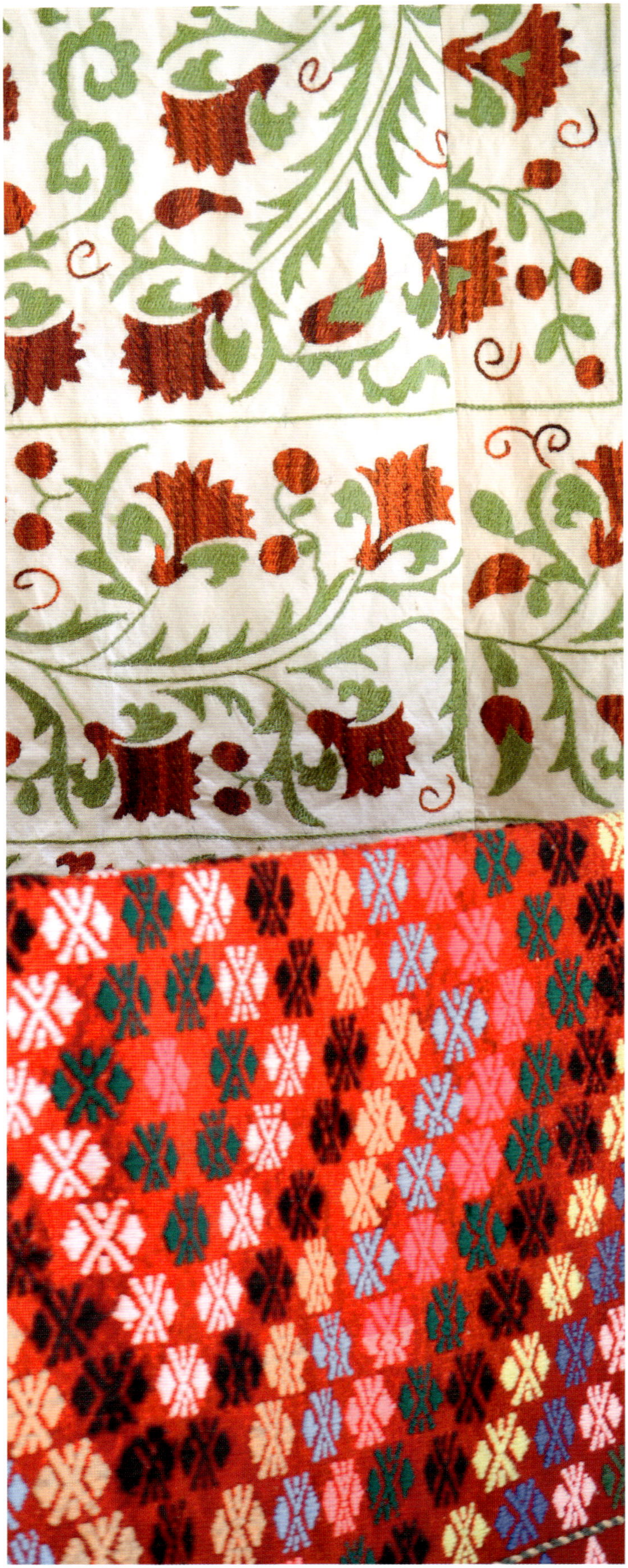

Custard Pie of Thessaloniki

Μπουγάτσα Θεσσαλονίκης

Serves 10
1.5 hours

I could not do a chapter on Northern Greece without a recipe for bougatsa. This is the most prominent breakfast served in Thessaloniki. Originally from Smyrna, this dish was called *sketi*, meaning "plain," with layers of filo pastry, hand-stretched and heavily brushed with oil and butter. This dish thereafter was introduced to Greece during the Ottoman Empire from the arrival of Greek refugees from Asia Minor and Cappadocia around the 1920s. Though this dish is traditionally made with filo pastry from scratch (and I'm a big fan of that), I also am realistic and understand that the majority of home cooks would prefer a store-bought pastry for efficiency and speed. In this case, a store-bought pastry will do just fine. Bougatsa can be made with semolina flour or with a combination of flour and cornstarch. Variations of bougatsa include a cheese-filled or a sweet custard filling with vanilla bean, encased by crispy buttered layers of filo generously dusted with icing sugar and cinnamon. Trust me, your guests will be stunned, and you will be delighted with the result. Bougatsa is always served in bite-size pieces.

140 g (0.3 lb. or 4.9 oz.) castor (superfine) sugar

70 g (0.15 lb. or 2.4 oz.) all-purpose flour

25 g (0.05 lb. or 0.88 oz.) cornstarch

4 whole eggs

700 mL (23.6 fl. oz.) whole milk

1 vanilla bean, deseeded

14 sheets store-bought filo pastry

140 g (0.3 lb. or 4.9 oz.) melted butter

Icing (confectioners) sugar to serve

Cinnamon powder to serve

In a bowl, add the sugar, flour, cornstarch, and eggs and whisk together. Set aside. In a saucepan and on medium heat, heat the milk and vanilla until hot. Whisk in the flour mixture, stirring constantly, until a think custard is achieved. This should be at boiling point. Remove from stove and place some cling film directly onto the custard (to avoid a skin forming). Set aside and prepare the filo.

Preheat oven to 160°C (320°F).

Butter a baking dish (30 cm x 25 cm or 11.8 in. x 9.8 in.). Place 7 sheets of filo pastry (allowing pastry to overhang over the baking dish), brushing butter on each layer. Pour in the custard. Enclose the overhanging pastry on the custard. Take the remaining 7 sheets of pastry and cut them to the size of the baking dish. Layer them on top, buttering each layer as you go. Pour any remaining butter over the top. Bake for 45 minutes or until golden brown. Serve warm with a generous sprinkle of cinnamon and icing sugar. This is best eaten the same day.

Muhallebi – Milk Pudding

Μαλεμπί

Serves 8
25 minutes, then 1 hour to set
Gluten-Free
Egg-Free

Obviously, this dish has an Arabic influence, and it was a loved dessert during the Ottoman Empire. It is a light, egg- and gluten-free dish that is simple to cook. What many call a "milk pudding," with a similar texture to a panacotta, *muhallebi* is cooked on the stovetop, then set aside to set. There are many alternatives to what accompaniment is best served with this pudding. The list really is endless. Crushed pistachios, rose petals, various spoon sweets, date syrup, orange blossom water, icing (confectioners) sugar—the list goes on. The actual pudding is not very sweet, so a sweet topping and crunch are necessary. An alternative to adding ouzo liquor would be rosewater, almond liquor, or mastiha powder (¼ teaspoon, ground), found in any European delicatessen. Mastic is the resin from the mastic tree, known as "tears of Chios," with a slight pine or cedar flavor. A small amount goes a long way. Overuse of this spice results in a bitter taste, so be very conservative with the quantities if you use it.

60 g (0.13 lb. or 2.1 oz.) castor (superfine) sugar

80 g (0.17 lb. or 2.8 oz.) cornstarch

20 g (0.04 lb. or 0.7 oz.) rice flour

1 L (33.81 fl. oz.) whole milk, divided

Pinch of salt

3 tablespoons ouzo liquor (if using almond essence or rosewater, use 2 tablespoons)

To serve:
Crushed pistachios

Edible rose petals (optional)

Sour cherry preserve (optional)

In a bowl, whisk together sugar, cornstarch, rice flour, 100 mL (3.38 fl. oz.) milk, pinch of salt, and ouzo liquor. Set aside. Place a saucepan on the stove, heating the remaining milk. Once milk is hot but not boiling, add the flour mixture, whisking continuously until the pudding has thickened. This should be at boiling point. Remove from heat and pour into eight small ramekins, dessert plates, or glasses. Place cling film directly onto each pudding, so as to avoid a skin forming. Allow to set approximately one hour (then place in the refrigerator until desired).

Serve topped with garnish of choice.

Eggplant Salad with a Garlic–Lemon Sauce

Μελιτζάνες με γιαούρτι

Serves 4
35 minutes
Gluten-Free

While I was researching produce in Thessaloniki, two vegetables stood out not only as abundantly grown but also as part of many recipes: the eggplant and capsicum. This dish combines both and is served as a great side. The mint and yogurt sauce adds a delightful zest and freshness. This can be made ahead of time. Fry the eggplant and capsicum, set aside, and two hours before serving, assemble and refrigerate. Flavors permeate the longer it is left in the fridge.

Oil for frying

1 large eggplant, cut into small cubes

1 green capsicum, sliced lengthwise

1 garlic clove, minced

½ cup yogurt

¼ cup olive oil

4 mint leaves, finely chopped

1 tablespoon lemon juice

1 teaspoon chopped dill

Salt to taste

½ a lemon, zested

Heat oil in shallow frying pan. Fry eggplant in batches until golden. Drain on paper towel and sprinkle salt over the top. Repeat with green capsicum. Place on a serving platter, preferably in one row.

Mix together the garlic, yogurt, ¼ cup olive oil, mint, lemon juice, dill, and salt. Pour over the eggplant and pepper. It can be served immediately (although it is preferable to serve cold, refrigerated for a minimum of 1–2 hours). Sprinkle with lemon zest and scatter some fresh mint over the top.

Stewed Aromatic Beef with Eggplant Mash

Serves 4
2.5 hours
Gluten-Free

Χουνκιάρ μπεγερντί

I was not persuaded by the sound of an eggplant mash with a beef/lamb stew until I read it on a menu, ordered it, and truly surprised myself at how delicious it really was. I had never even read about it prior to that moment, let alone ever eaten it. I took my first bite into a soft, cheesy charred eggplant puree accompanied by a wonderfully spiced meat stew that just melted in my mouth. It was very decadent and intense in flavor. This dish originated in Constantinople in the year AD 1632. Directly translated, the name of this dish means, "the sultan was satisfied." Story has it once again that the sultan ate of this and was overly satisfied, and thus, we now have hünkâr beğendi. Originally, this dish was made with eggplants and cheese as the base, but the Greeks adapted it by adding a béchamel sauce to the smoked eggplants. Whether the sultan ate this or not, I guarantee that you will be satisfied and so pleasantly surprised at how delicious it really is. Stew can be prepared up to a day ahead; otherwise, prepare the stew as you wait for the eggplants to cook.

To make the stew: In a large casserole, place the oil, onion, and sugar. On medium heat, cook until soft and translucent. Add the meat and brown well on all sides. Add the wine and allow to cook for 2 minutes. Add all the remaining ingredients. Cover and allow to simmer on low for 45–55 minutes. Taste and adjust seasoning if needed. The meat should be tender and the sauce reduced to a little over half in the pot.

Place the whole eggplants directly onto a gas burner or, preferably, on a grill with coals. The aim here is to have a smoky taste permeate the eggplants so that the mash has a smoky flavor. Cook the eggplants until they are black and blistering, about 30 minutes. Alternatively, place the eggplants on a baking tray and bake at 200°C (392°F) for 40 minutes or until blistered and soft. Once cooked and still hot, place into a bowl covered with cling film. This will help the skins peel more easily. After 5 minutes, remove cling film from the bowl and peel away the skin. If there are a few charred bits remaining, that's okay. It adds flavor to the mash. Place the peeled eggplants back in the bowl, mashing them slightly (or pulse 2–3 times in a food processor, being careful to not overpulse). Mix through lemon juice so that the eggplants don't blacken from oxidation. Set aside.

Next, make the white sauce. On a medium heat, add the oil and flour to a pot. Whisk for 1 minute to incorporate. Add milk and whisk continually until the sauce has thickened (should take 5–10 minutes). Take off heat and add cheese, nutmeg, salt, and pepper. Mix together. Add the mashed eggplant and mix through to incorporate. Taste and adjust seasoning if needed.

To serve, heat the stew. Place the mash onto a large, flat platter and then top the center with the stew. Otherwise, serve individually. Best eaten with a side salad and freshly baked bread to mop up the juices.

*See description of Kasseri cheese in glossary. It can be substituted with mozzarella cheese.

2 medium-size eggplants, whole

¼ lemon, juiced

Stew:
¼ cup olive oil

1 brown onion, diced

1 teaspoon castor (superfine) sugar

500 g (1.1 lb. or 17.6 oz.) boneless stewing lamb or beef (shoulder, shank, or leg), cubed into bite-size pieces

½ cup red wine

1 tablespoon tomato paste

1 cup tomato puree

1 tablespoon cinnamon powder

1 teaspoon clove powder

1 bay leaf

4 allspice berries (pimento)

Salt and pepper to taste

1 cup water

White Sauce for Eggplant Mash:
4 tablespoons olive oil

6 tablespoons all-purpose flour

2 cups whole milk

½ cup grated kasseri cheese*

1 teaspoon nutmeg powder

Salt and pepper to taste

Stewed Aromatic Beef with Eggplant Mash, page 65.

Revani
Yogurt and Semolina Cake

Παραδοσιακό ραβανί Βέροιας

Serves 30 pieces
1 hour plus overnight refrigeration

This cake comes under the category of *siropiasta* in the Greek cuisine, meaning "syrup-drenched." The cake must remain moist; therefore, do not be tempted to reduce the sugar—it needs all the syrup! Just have a smaller piece with a dollop of yogurt to cut through the sweetness. There is a beautiful tartness from the yogurt and the zest in the batter. It is best made a day before, allowing the syrup to permeate throughout the whole cake. Serve cold directly from the fridge. It will keep up to five days covered and refrigerated. There are many variations throughout Greece, with the use of almond meal, butter, and spices. This dessert is from the northern region of Veria, with few and simple ingredients, being the semolina flour, oil, yogurt, and lemon. The exact origin is not documented, although there are similar desserts in the Middle East, Egypt (basbousa, made with coconut) and in Istanbul (using a rose or orange blossom syrup). Food scholars suggest that the Istanbul poet Revani in the sixteenth century may have developed the original dessert, seeing that he extensively wrote about food. Hence the name.

Syrup:
3 cups castor (superfine) sugar
750 mL (25.36 fl. oz.) water
3 strips lemon peel

Cake batter:
250 mL (8.45 fl. oz.) light olive oil
50 g (0.11 lb. or 1.76 oz.) castor (superfine) sugar
1 cup yogurt
4 whole eggs
½ teaspoon vanilla sugar or 1 vanilla bean, deseeded
5 lemons, zested
1½ teaspoons baking powder
340 g (0.74 lb. or 11.9 oz.) coarse semolina flour*
125 g (0.27 lb. or 4.4 oz.) all-purpose plain flour

Place all the syrup ingredients into a pot and bring to a boil. Lower heat and simmer for 7 minutes, then set aside to come to room temperature. Preheat oven to 170°C (338°F). Line a square loaf tin 24cm (9 in.) with parchment paper.

In a mixer, beat the oil with the sugar. Add the yogurt and the eggs one at a time, beating well after each addition. Add vanilla, lemon zest, baking powder, semolina flour, and, slowly, a spoonful at a time of the plain flour. Mix until combined. Pour mixture into loaf tin, flattening the top with a palette knife or spoon and bake for 30–35 minutes or until a skewer inserted comes out clean. Immediately pour the cooled syrup onto the hot cake with a ladle. It will seem like a lot of syrup, but it will slowly sop it up. Allow the cake to come to room temperature, then cover and refrigerate overnight. Slice and serve with a dollop of yogurt and caramelized lemon slices (available from specialized delicatessens).

*The semolina flour must be the coarse variety, otherwise the cake will become too soggy.

Tip: You could also top this with a lemon cream. Place 300 mL (10.14 fl. oz.) thickened (heavy) cream, together with 4 tablespoons lemon juice, 2 tablespoons icing (confectioners) sugar, and zest of one lemon, into a mixer. Beat until thickened. Serve with the cake.

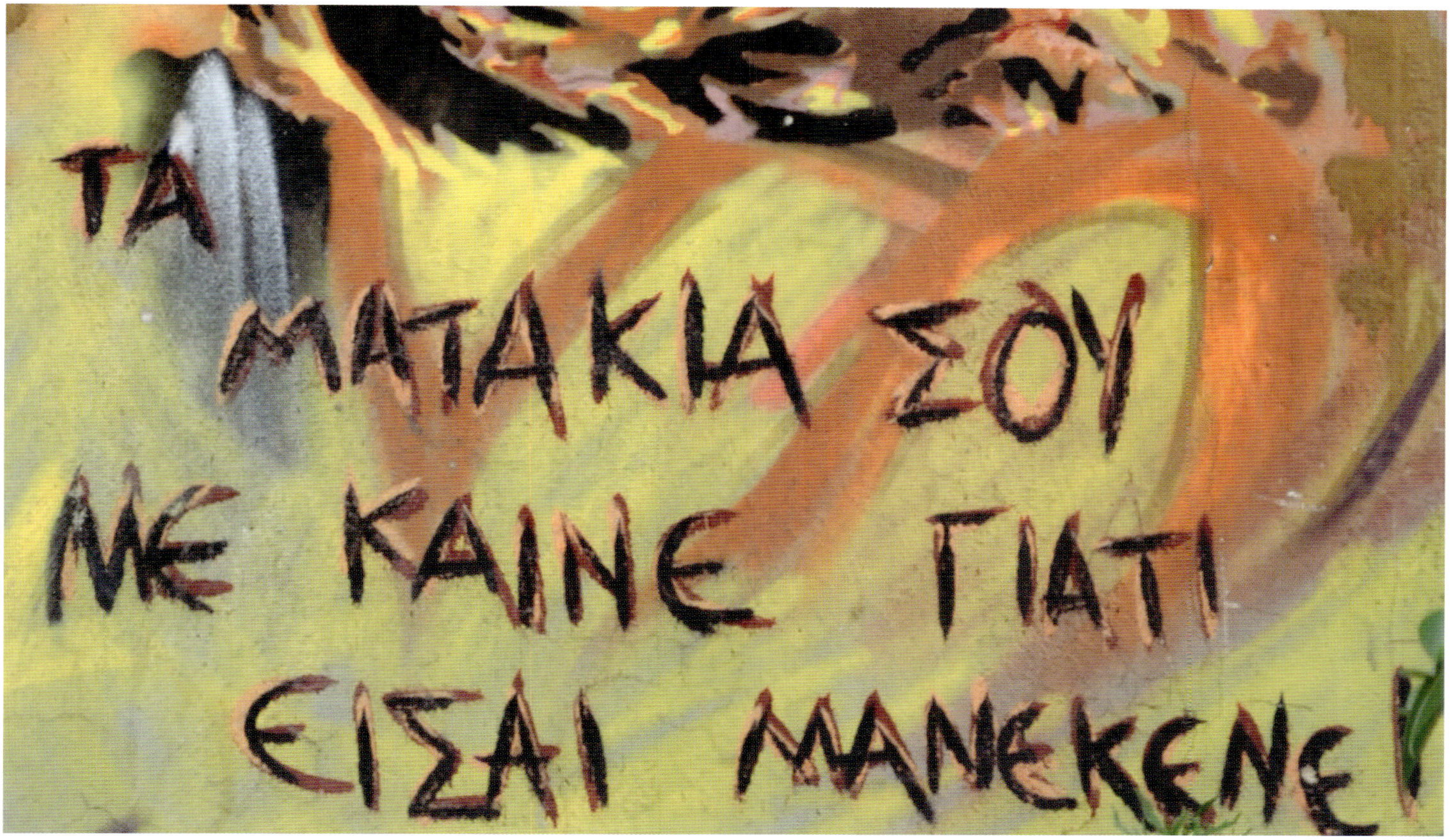

ΤΑ ΜΑΤΑΚΙΑ ΣΟΥ ΜΕ ΚΑΙΝΕ ΓΙΑΤΙ ΕΙΣΑΙ ΜΑΝΕΚΕΝΕ!

Baked Feta Cheese

Φέτα μπουγιουρντί

Serves 3
30 minutes
Gluten-Free

The smell and taste of soft, gooey baked feta, simmered in a parcel or baked in an earthenware dish with plenty of olive oil, oregano, and a few other simple ingredients, is an absolute palate pleaser. This appetizer has its roots in Thessaloniki, although nowadays it is served throughout Greece. Ensure that you use a good-quality feta cheese. Unwrap the parcel and serve directly from the parchment paper. If you have a fancy dinner party, a small parcel for each guest is appealing.

- 150 g (0.33 lb. or 5.29 oz.) block feta cheese
- ¼ onion, sliced
- ½ red or green capsicum sliced
- 4 cherry tomatoes, halved
- 1 teaspoon dried oregano
- ¼ teaspoon dried chili flakes
- ½ cup olive oil

Preheat oven to 200°C (390°F).

Cut a piece of foil and parchment paper (20 cm or 7.9 in. square). Place the paper on top of the foil. Place the block of feta cheese in the center of the paper. Layer the onion, capsicum, and tomato on top. Sprinkle the oregano and chili flakes and drizzle with the olive oil. Wrap the foil to enclose the feta, ensuring the juices won't seep out. Place on a baking tray and bake for 25–30 minutes or until feta is soft and the veggies have softened. Serve hot with crusty bread.

Alternatively, all the ingredients can be placed in an earthenware dish and baked covered for 20 minutes, or until all the vegetables and feta have softened.

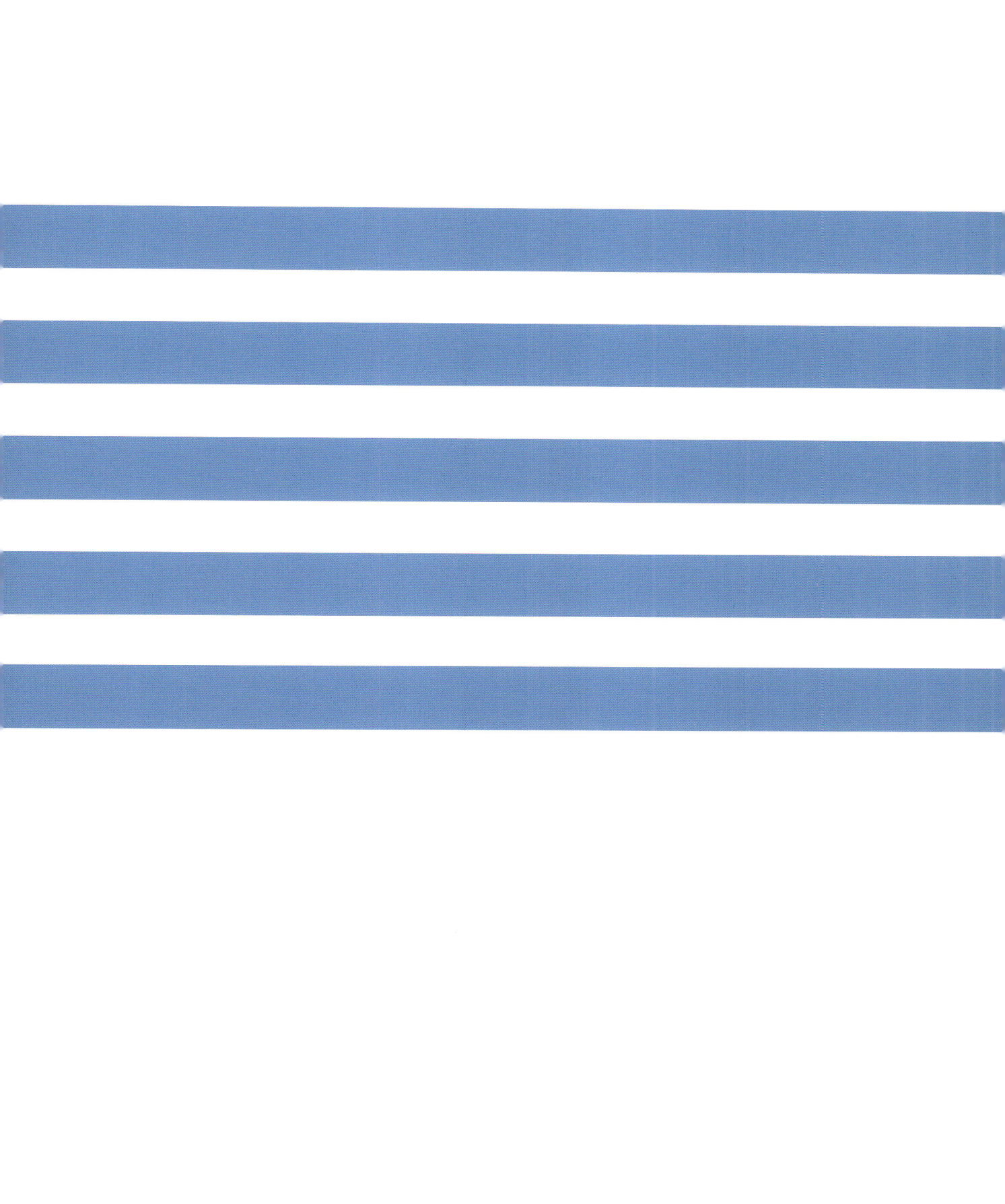

Peloponnese
Τρίτο 03

The Peloponnese is situated in the southernmost part of mainland Greece. It is the region known for the first Olympic Games held at Olympia, for the Spartans, and for the birthplace and grandeur of Greek heroes such as Herakles, Agamemnon, and Eleni. We read mythologies like *The Odyssey* and *The Iliad*, and yet this region goes far beyond legends and stories! Roam through the Peloponnese, and one thing will be undoubtedly noticeable—the region's most precious crop, the *olive tree*! Nothing epitomizes the Greek cuisine more so than olive oil. Remove olive oil from the Greek gastronomy, and half of it is instantly gone! It is also the most eaten raw ingredient in Greece! It is the distinguished ingredient in Greek cookery and the essence of the Peloponnesian cuisine! It is no surprise that most dishes from this region have an excessive amount of olive oil, which is rich in flavor and nutrients.

This region can stand alone in terms of produce. It has plenty of all one needs to retain a Mediterranean balanced diet. Surrounded by land and sea, this region has copious amounts of seafood and a plethora of crops inclusive of the exquisite grape vines, dark and light raisins, lemons, artichokes, and oranges. Pork and rabbit are the favored meats. Homemade pastas, known as *hilopites*, pasta pies, and wheat products are ever arraying the tables of the Peloponnese. Wild greens are picked and are added to many meals, topped with a lemon juice and egg emulsion *avgolemono*. The art of smoking foods was a way to preserve pork, such as the classic *pasto* (salted meat) with sage. Aromatic plants such as dill and fennel were and are still commonly used. Desserts are primarily sweetened with honey and petimezi (grape must), while a prevalent sweet, *diples*, are fried in extra-virgin olive oil, giving the pastry a beautiful golden color and wonderful flavor. So indulge in the meals and desserts that highlight the region's most prominent ingredient—olive oil!

The Aromatic South

Spaghetti and Cheese Pie

Μακαρονόπιτα

Serves 30 pieces
1 hour 20 minutes

Everyone knows the famous macaroni and cheese bake; well, this is a macaroni (spaghetti) and cheese pie! Versions of a sort are cooked throughout Greece, but the cooks of the Peloponnese pride themselves in making this as their take on the traditional *pastitsio*. Encased in homemade filo dough, the tubular macaroni is submerged in Greek cheeses, milk, and eggs and liberally coated with olive oil. The pastry remains crispy and crunchy, while the interior remains moist and soft. This is a comfort pie at its best! For that extra flavor, add some chopped olives and roasted capsicums to the filling. It is best eaten at room temperature.

Pastry:
2 cups all-purpose plain flour

2 tablespoons olive oil

1 tablespoon salt

1 teaspoon white or red wine vinegar

1 cup warm water

Corn flour (starch) for rolling out filo pastry

½ cup olive oil for brushing pastry layers and top

Prepare filo pastry. Place all the ingredients into a large bowl. Bring together with a wooden spoon, then tip onto a floured benchtop and knead until soft and smooth. Add more flour, if needed, or water, if it is too dry. This should take a few minutes. Cover and rest for a minimum of 25 minutes.

Preheat oven to 190°C (374°F).

Boil the pasta until al dente, as per instructions on the packet. Drain, place in a bowl, and drizzle the olive oil to inhibit the pasta from sticking together. Allow the pasta to cool slightly. In another bowl, add the eggs, milk, and a pinch of salt and pepper, whisking together to combine. Pour this onto the cooked pasta. Mix to ensure the pasta is coated with the egg mixture. Add the grated cheese and the crumbled feta. Mix and set aside.

Take the dough and divide into four pieces. Dust a workbench with corn flour and place one piece of dough on the bench. Dust more corn flour on top, and with a *plasti* (thin wooden dowel), start to roll out the dough into a very large circle. You can use a square tin, but you must ensure the pastry is rolled out a little larger than the tray you use. It must have an overhang. In this case, I used a circular tray size 37 cm (14.56 in.).

Line the baking tray with parchment paper and place the first piece of filo pastry. Drizzle some olive oil on top and repeat with the second sheet. Pour the filling onto the pastry and fold over the overhang to hold the filling and keep it from seeping out. Roll out the third sheet of pastry and place it on top, scrunching all the extra overlay on the top to create a ruffled effect. Drizzle oil on top and repeat with the last sheet of filo. Drizzle olive oil on top and score with a sharp knife into desired squares or slices.

Bake for 35 minutes or until golden. Serve warm or at room temperature.

*Kasseri and kefalograviera cheese available at European delicatessens. Parmesan cheese can be used as a substitute.

Filling:
250 g (0.55 lb. or 8.81 oz.) tubular pasta

3 tablespoons olive oil

4 whole eggs

2 cups whole milk

Pinch of salt and pepper

300 g (0.66 lb. or 10.5 oz.) feta cheese, crumbled

2 cups kasseri or kefalograviera cheese* grated

Spaghetti and Cheese Pie, page 77.

Fried Pastry with Walnuts, Cinnamon and Honey

Δίπλες

Serves 40 pieces
1.5 hours

The name *diples* comes from the word *diplono*, meaning "to fold," and these are a specialty of the Peloponnese region. They are somewhat labor-intensive but well worth the effort. I like to double the batch. This is an egg dough that gets rolled out very thinly and fried in hot olive oil. As it fries, it sizzles and creates a crackly, airy, and puffy dough. Carefully, it is shaped into a cylinder, then set out to dry. Some versions get dunked into hot syrup immediately. This recipe does not, so that they remain fresher for longer. They get served with runny honey, a sprinkling of cinnamon powder, and crushed walnuts! Place the diples in a bowl, covered with a tea towel, for up to six weeks. Do not store in a container, as they will go soft.

3 whole eggs

3 yolks

1/3 cup castor (superfine) sugar

1/8 cup ouzo liquor

2 tablespoons baking powder

1/6 cup whole milk

2–3 cups all-purpose flour

Light olive oil for frying

Honey to serve

1 cup ground walnuts

Cinnamon powder to dust

In a stand mixer with the whisk attached, add the whole eggs and yolks. Whisk to combine. With the machine running, add sugar, ouzo, baking powder, and milk. Remove the whisk and use the dough hook attachment. Add flour (the amount of flour will vary, so add only cupsful at a time) until a soft dough that doesn't stick to your hands is achieved. Remove the dough from the mixer and knead the dough on the bench after the third cup of flour is added. The dough is ready once it stops sticking to your hands. Roll into a ball, wrap the dough in cling film, and refrigerate for 30 minutes.

Divide the dough into six pieces. Take one piece at a time and place through a pasta machine from settings 1 to 7. Place onto a floured bench, and with a flat or serrated knife, cut into 15 cm (6 in.) lengths and 7 cm (2.7 in.) widths. Half-fill a frying pan with oil. Heat oil well. To test if the oil is hot enough, place a small piece of pastry in it, and if the pastry sizzles and rises, it is ready.

Gently drop one piece of dough into the oil, and immediately it should start to puff up and sizzle. It will take at least 3–4 diples to get the ideal temperature and technique, so don't worry if the first few don't turn out correct. Very quickly turn the dough piece upside down and allow it to puff up (should take 2–3 seconds). With two forks, gently but quickly roll the pastry into a cylinder. You want a very light golden color to be achieved. Hold it down for a few seconds, then release and allow it to get golden. Remove and place on a paper towel to drain. Repeat with the remaining pastry. Serve diples individually, drizzled with honey and sprinkled with walnuts and cinnamon powder.

Olive Oil and Orange Cookies

Κουλουράκια

Serves 45 pieces
1 hour 30 minutes
Dairy-Free
Egg-Free

These circular cookies are egg- and dairy-free, flavored with freshly squeezed orange juice and cinnamon. They can be made without a stand mixer. Koulourakia are in every sweet shop throughout Greece and most probably made in every household, especially through the Easter season. They are not super sweet and are a great accompaniment to tea or coffee. This recipe is true to the roots of the Peloponnese produce, priding oranges and olive oil. They are crispy and light!

120 mL (4.05 fl. oz.) orange juice, freshly squeezed

½ teaspoon baking soda

200 mL (6.76 fl. oz.) olive oil

1 cup castor (superfine) sugar

1 orange, zested

60 mL (2.02 fl. oz.) orange liquor (optional)

1 teaspoon baking powder

1 teaspoon cinnamon powder

600 g (1.32 lb. or 21.1 oz.) all-purpose flour

2 cups sesame, raw

Preheat oven to 180°C (365°F).

In a bowl, place the orange juice and baking soda. Stir to combine. It will fizzle and foam. Set aside.

Place the olive oil and sugar in a bowl. Whisk to combine. Add the zest, liquor, baking powder, cinnamon, and orange juice mixture, mixing well to combine. With a wooden spoon, slowly incorporate the flour little by little, being careful not to overmix. Add more flour, if needed. The dough must be soft but not sticky. Allow the dough to rest for 20 minutes.

Place the sesame into a bowl and set aside. Line a baking tray with parchment paper. Take a piece of dough weighing 25 g (0.05 lb. or 0.88 oz.). Roll out into a rope length no longer than 13 cm (5 in.). Join the ends together to make a circle cookie. Dip into the sesame to coat the cookie. Place on the tray and repeat with the remaining dough. Bake for 35 minutes or until golden brown. Allow to cool. Place in an airtight container. They will keep for 1–2 weeks.

Tapenade Olive Dip

Πάστα ελιάς

Serves 1 jar
10 minutes
Gluten-Free

Go to the region of Kalamata, and the olive that you will eat will be the *Kalamon* variety! They are unquestionably eaten day-to-day at a Greek table, and the Peloponnese people pride themselves in the export and consumption of these olives. They are preserved in red wine vinegar and olive oil. The large, almond-shaped, purply-black, plump olives are very meaty and balanced in their acidity. Classified as a fruit, the olive is formed from the "ovary of the olive flower." The pit (known as a seed-bearing structure), if planted, can grow into a tree. Kalamata olives cannot be harvested green and therefore are handpicked to avoid any bruising. Ever so versatile, these olives array an antipasto menu, add flavor to Greek salads, and make a delicious olive dip. This is very easy to make and very addictive, so you may want to double the quantity.

2 cups Kalamata olives, pitted

2 tablespoons capers

1 lemon, juiced

1 cup extra-virgin olive oil

5 brined anchovies*

Salt and pepper to taste

Place olives and capers into a food processor. Process to combine until mixture is a coarse paste. Add the remaining ingredients and pulse again to combine well. Taste and adjust seasoning if needed. Refrigerate in a sealed jar for up to one week.

*Do not be tempted to omit anchovies if you do not like them. Once the dip is combined, you will not be able to taste any fishiness. It is a crucial ingredient to give this dip its beautiful flavor.

Wine-Cooked Rooster with Egg Pasta

Κόκορας κρασάτος με χυλοπίτες

Serves 6 - 8
2.5 hours
Gluten-Free

Hilopites are a very small, square egg pasta traditionally made by hand. Made in the summer months in preparation for winter cooking, these dried pasta squares are customarily in every Peloponnese household. Long linguine pasta is made, then carefully cut by hand into small squares. Long before refrigeration, as a way to preserve eggs and milk (there are also egg- and milk-free varieties), this pasta was the go-to solution for mothers and grandmothers to feed their large families. Always on hand, this pasta was used in soups, stews, and pies, making it a very versatile way to prepare meals. These days, hilopites are readily available online and in Mediterranean delicatessens. For this recipe, buy store-bought hilopites. This is a recipe with few ingredients all made in one casserole. As this stew cooks, it releases an intense aroma from the cinnamon and clove. The addition of grape molasses gives the dish an overall sweetness that balances well with the spices and wine.

1 cup olive oil

1 whole rooster, cut into 8–9 pieces (preferably organic)*

Salt and pepper to taste

1 medium onion, diced

2 garlic cloves, minced

1 cup white wine

2 cups tomato puree

3 tablespoons tomato paste

2 tablespoons grape molasses, otherwise known as petimezi (optional)**

1 teaspoon paprika powder

7 whole cloves

1 cinnamon quill

In a large casserole dish, heat the olive oil on medium heat. Add the rooster pieces and season with salt and pepper. Brown the meat well on both sides. Remove the meat and set aside. To the casserole, add the onion and garlic, sautéing until very soft and caramelized. Add the meat back in. To this, add the wine and allow to cook off for 1 minute. Add the tomato puree, paste, molasses, paprika, cloves, and cinnamon quill. Stir to mix in well. Add boiled water, ensuring that everything is submerged. Allow to simmer on low for 2 hours.†

Check for seasoning (you want it to be a little saltier than normal—once the pasta is added, it will be fine).

Remove the cooked rooster from the casserole. Cover and set aside. Measure the stock remaining in the pot. You should have around 1 L (1,000 mL). Pour stock back into the casserole dish, adding an additional 1½ cups water. Bring to a full boil. Add the pasta, stirring well so that it doesn't stick to the bottom of the pot. Cook for 10–15 minutes or until the pasta is cooked. If it is drying out, add a little more water. It should not be dry nor too soupy. Once cooked, return the rooster to the pan and mix through.

Serve immediately with some mizithra cheese.

*Get your butcher to portion the rooster.

**Hilopites, mizithra cheese, and grape molasses are available at international grocers. Parmesan cheese can be substituted for mizithra cheese.

†Tip: You could use a pressure cooker if you are short on time.

4 cups boiled water

500 g (1.1 lb. or 17.6 oz.) hilopites (square egg pasta) **

Mizithra cheese, grated, to serve**

"Educating the mind without educating the heart is no education at all"

— Aristotle

Wine-Cooked Rooster with Egg Pasta, page 87.

Spinach Risotto

Σπανακόρυζο

Serves 4
30-40 mintues
Gluten-Free

Spanakorizo is translated "spinach and rice" and is one of the most classic vegetarian dishes in the Greek cuisine. Spinach is cooked with rice, lemon, onions, and olive oil. This dish is simple in its execution and super delicious and nutritious in its flavor and benefit! There are two classic ways to make this meal: "white," meaning plain with only lemon (as below), or "red," with the addition of tomatoes. It can be served with crumbled feta cheese or simply on its own with a piece of fish or protein.

½ cup olive oil

½ cup onion or spring onion, finely chopped

¼ cup leeks, finely chopped

1 garlic clove, minced

1 teaspoon thyme, chopped

1 cup arborio or risotto rice

1 cup white wine

2 cups boiled water

250 g (0.55 lb. or 8.81 oz.) spinach leaves, washed and roughly chopped

1–2 lemons (to taste), zested and juiced

Salt and pepper to taste

Sauté onion and leek in the olive oil until soft. Add garlic, thyme, and rice and continue to sauté until the rice is translucent. Add wine and cook for about 3 minutes, allowing the wine to evaporate. Pour 2 cups of boiled water. Place a lid on top and allow to simmer on low heat for approximately 10–15 minutes or until rice is cooked. Place the spinach in a bowl and add a pinch of salt.

Gently scrunch it with your hands, draining any liquid so that once added to the rice, it won't go green. Remove the pan from heat and add spinach (do not add earlier, as the rice will go green). Add a little more boiled water if the consistency is too dry. Season well and add lemon juice and zest. Mix to incorporate.

Serve immediately with a side of feta cheese (or crumbled over the top) and a lemon wedge.

Tip: It will continue to thicken slightly. If you like a juicier risotto, add a little more boiled water at the end.

Grape Must Pudding

Μουσταλευριά

Serves 6
15 minutes plus 1 hour (minimum refrigeration)
Gluten-Free
Dairy-Free

This is a soft, gelatinous pudding rich in antioxidants and vitamins. The star of this dessert is the grape must, otherwise known as *petimezi* (an intense grape syrup). The name comes from two words in Greek: *mousto*, meaning "must," and *alevri*, meaning "flour." There is no added sugar, and it is dairy- and gluten-free. I have used cornstarch as the alternative to flour, as I find it is a little lighter in texture. Always garnish with crushed walnuts and a sprinkle of cinnamon powder. It can be served as a slice (ensure it has been refrigerated overnight) or in cups or small bowls. It is best eaten cold.

1 cup concentrated grape syrup (petimezi)*

2½ cups water, divided

6 tablespoon corn flour (cornstarch)

50 g (0.11 lb. or 1.76 oz.) crushed walnuts

Sesame seeds, toasted (optional)

Cinnamon powder

In a pot, bring the petimezi and 2 cups water to a boil. It will turn into a light brown color but will darken again as it thickens. Reduce to medium heat. Combine the remaining water and cornstarch, whisking to remove any lumps. Add this to the pot, whisking continuously until it has thickened and starts to bubble and boil, roughly 5–8 minutes. Remove from heat and place in individual bowls, small cups, or in a shallow baking dish (if you prefer slices).

Allow to cool completely (or refrigerate overnight if serving in slices). To serve, scatter walnuts and sesame (optional) and sprinkle cinnamon powder over the top.

*See description of Petimezi in glossary. Petimezi (grape must) is readily available from European delicatessens. Ensure it is as natural as possible, without any added chemicals.

Grape Must and Orange Cookies

Μουστοκούλουρα

Serves 50 cookies
1 hour
Dairy-Free
Egg-Free

This is another wonderful recipe using petimezi (see previous recipe) and orange. These cookies are easy to assemble using only one mixing bowl. Though they are not the most attractive cookies, be assured the flavor is amazing! Gently spiced with cinnamon and clove, these taste like a combination of gingerbread and soft and chewy biscotti. There are no eggs, no sugar, and no dairy, making it a versatile cookie for anyone with allergies. This dough must not be overworked, as it has no eggs, which therefore means the olive oil can separate from the dough more easily. You do not want this. Store in a glass container for weeks on end—remember that as each day passes, the taste intensifies!

1 cup grape molasses (petimezi)*

1 cup olive oil

170 mL (5.74 fl. oz) orange juice, freshly squeezed

2 oranges, zested

¼ cup runny honey

1½ teaspoons ground cinnamon powder

½ teaspoon ground cloves

1½ teaspoons baking powder

1 teaspoon baking soda

1/3 cup currants

750–800 g (1.16–1.76 lb. or 26–28 oz.) all-purpose plain flour, sifted

In a large bowl, place the molasses, oil, orange juice, orange zest, honey, cinnamon powder, clove powder, baking powder, and baking soda. Whisk to combine well. Leave it 5 minutes to slightly foam up (reaction of soda with orange juice). To this add the currants and three-quarters of the sifted flour. Gently mix with a wooden spoon, being careful not to overmix. Keep adding the remaining flour until a pliable dough that does not stick to your hands is achieved. It will be very soft and a little gluey to the hands.

Preheat oven to 175°C (350°F).

Take a handful of dough (weighing 30 g or 0.06 lb. or 1.05 oz.) and roll between your palms to create a unified ball. Then gently roll into a snake shape (12 cm or 4.72 in. length), then press together and join ends. Place onto a lined baking tray and bake for 20–25 minutes or until slightly golden on the bottom side of the cookie. Yes, the bottom side will give you the correct indication that the cookie is cooked enough. They will feel slightly soft, but once cooled, they will harden. Allow to cool and keep in an airtight container.

*See description of Petimezi in glossary. Petimezi (grape must) is readily available from European delicatessens. Ensure it is as natural as possible, without any added chemicals.

Roasted Goat with Dill and Artichokes

Κατσικάκι Φρικασέ

Serves 5
(2 artichokes each)
2 hours
Gluten-Free

The Peloponnese region is the home of where most artichokes are grown in Greece. In the spring, when artichokes are in season, they are cooked fresh into one-pot meals, and many are cleaned and placed in the freezer for meals in the winter. It is a little tedious to rightly prepare the artichokes but well worth the effort. They can also be eaten as a vegetarian dish see recipe *Braised Artichokes with Baby Peas*.

10 artichokes, cleaned and halved (frozen will also work)

2½ lemons, divided

1 baby goat leg or leg of lamb, cut into portions (1-2 kg or 2.2 lb. or 35.27 oz.)

7 whole garlic cloves

Salt and pepper to taste

5 medium potatoes, peeled and quartered

1 cup dill, chopped

2 spring onions, chopped

2 tablespoons tomato paste

2 cups tomato puree

¾ cup olive oil

2 lemons juiced

1 cup water

Preheat the oven to 190°C (374°F).

Prepare the artichokes by slicing the top of each artichoke, then, starting from the base, remove the outer petals until half the artichoke remains. Cut off the excess stem or tail, leaving about 2 cm (an inch). With a teaspoon, remove the center core (it is fuzzy and called the "choke"). Cut the artichoke in half and immediately add to a bowl of water with the juice of half a lemon. This prevents the artichoke from oxidizing and changing color.

Take a large baking dish and place the goat leg in the center. Make incisions in the goat leg and add slices of garlic, then season well with salt and pepper. Now add the potatoes, dill, artichokes, and onions. In a small bowl, mix the tomato paste with the tomato puree to dissolve well. Pour into the baking tray. Drizzle the olive oil and the juice of the lemons, then add some more pepper and salt and 1 cup water. Cover and bake for 2 hours, then uncover and allow to brown another 20 minutes. If juices are drying out, add one cup of water.

Serve warm with some fronds of extra dill.

Pork and Celery Stew with an Egg and Lemon Emulsion

Χοιρινό με σέλινο αυγολέμονο

Serves 4-6
1.5 hours
Gluten-Free

This is one of those dishes that you need to trust the author that it will be delicious! This is peasant food at its finest and a tasty meal. Trust me on this one—you need to try this recipe. Celery and pork are the heroes of this dish. Foraged in the autumn months, celery grows wild in the Peloponnese. The final pouring of the lemon and egg emulsion adds creaminess and tang to the overall dish.

1 kg (2.2 lb. or 35.2 oz.) pork neck, cut into bite-size pieces

½ cup all-purpose flour

¾ cup olive oil, divided

Salt and pepper to taste

1 medium onion, sliced

2 spring onions, chopped

½ cup leek, chopped

1 cup white wine

900 mL (30.43 fl. oz.) water

150 g (0.33 lb. or 5.29 oz.) celery, leaves only

½ cup dill, chopped

Lemon emulsion:
1 whole egg

2 lemons, zested and juiced

Wash the pork well and allow to strain in a colander. Add the flour and shake to coat all the meat. In a heavy-based pan, heat ½ cup olive oil. When hot, add the pork, browning well on all sides. Season generously with salt and pepper. Remove meat and add the remaining ¼ cup olive oil. To this, add the onion, spring onions, and leek, sautéing until soft. Place the browned meat into the pot and pour in wine, cooking for 3 minutes, then add the water.

Cover and cook on medium heat for about 40–50 minutes or until the pork is cooked through. Add the celery and dill and continue to cook covered for another 15 minutes. Then turn the heat off and keep the lid on.

In a bowl, add the egg, zest, and lemon juice. Whisk to combine. Now take 2 ladles full of stock from the saucepan and add to the egg mixture, whisking quickly so that the eggs don't curdle. Pour this over the meat and greens while quickly stirring to mix through. Serve with some crusty bread.

Stewed Sweet Peas

Αρακάς λαδερός

Serves 2-3
35-40 minutes
Gluter-Free

The exact translation of this dish is "oily peas." It may not sound like a dish you want to try, but I can guarantee you, once you have tasted this, you will have a bookmark on this page. It is a very quick and simple meal to make. Who does not have frozen peas in the freezer, some olive oil, and seasonings on hand any time of the week! I eat peas often. I toss them in salads, add them to stews, and regularly make this dish. It is one of those dishes that can be served as a meze or a side to a main or even eaten on its own with a good helping of freshly baked bread and crumbled feta cheese. This is best cooked in a wide sauté pan. Once cooked, the oil surfaces to the top, leaving a glossy stream of liquid that screams out, "mop me up!" Flavors develop, and the peas get sweeter the longer they are stewed. This dish can be made with the addition of beef, although I prefer this vegetarian version. Many variations include red peppers, carrots, and potatoes. In many regions in Greece, it is made with no tomato but rather olive oil, herbs, and lemon juice. Both are delicious!

½ cup olive oil

½ medium onion, diced

2 tablespoons tomato paste

400 g (0.88 lb. or 14.1 oz.) frozen peas

Salt and pepper to taste

1 teaspoon castor (superfine) sugar

2 tablespoons fresh dill, chopped

In a sauté pan, heat the olive oil. Add the onion and sauté until soft and translucent. Add the tomato paste and mix to incorporate into the oil. Add the peas, salt, pepper, sugar, and dill. Pour enough boiled water to just cover the peas. Place a lid on and allow to simmer on low for 30–40 minutes, or until the water has evaporated and oil has surfaced to the top.

Can be eaten immediately or at room temperature.

Serve with a sprinkling of fresh dill and a splash of olive oil.

Braised Artichokes with Baby Peas

Αγκινάρες με αρακά

Serves 6
1 hour
Gluten-Free*

This braised artichoke and pea dish depicts springtime in the Peloponnese! The artichoke period is brief, so frozen artichokes are a great alternative for when fresh are not in season. Sweet frozen baby peas are also great for this dish! If using tender, young baby artichokes, just slice down the middle (removing choke), then cook as per the recipe. The lemon adds a delicious zing and pairs wonderfully with the peas and potatoes.

- 1 cup olive oil
- 1 large onion, diced
- 2 small carrots, sliced
- 3 potatoes, peeled and quartered
- 1 tablespoon all-purpose flour*
- 8 artichoke hearts, fresh or frozen**
- 1 cup white wine
- Salt and pepper to taste
- ¼ cup dill, finely chopped
- 2½ cups frozen peas
- 2 lemons, juiced
- 1 whole egg, separated

In a wide sauté pan and on medium heat, cook the onion with the olive oil until soft. Add carrots, potatoes, and flour, cooking for 2 minutes to incorporate the flour. Add artichokes, wine, salt and pepper, dill, and peas and mix to combine. Cover everything with boiled water, lower the heat, and place a lid on the pan and cook for 40–50 minutes or until the artichokes and potatoes are cooked. If the liquid is driving out too quickly, add one cup of water and continue cooking. You want a thickened sauce to be in the pan. Lower heat until you make the egg and lemon emulsion.

Beat the egg white until white and thick. Add the yolk and whisk to combine. Add the lemon juice and whisk well to incorporate. Add 4 tablespoons of the liquid from the pan, ensuring you beat it quickly so the egg does not curdle. Pour this mixture over the cooked dish, tilting the pan so that the mixture gets distributed throughout. Turn heat off immediately and allow it to stand 5 minutes before serving.

*Use corn flour (cornstarch) in place of flour for a gluten-free version.

**To use fresh artichokes trim the stems. Remove outer leaves and cut the top off. The heart (otherwise known as the furry part, or choke) needs to be scooped out, and then they need to be placed in a bowl of lemon water until required. You will also find that fresh artichokes need a little longer to cook.

Pork Stew with Peppers

Χοιρινό κοκκινιστό με πιπεριές

Serves 6
1.5 hours
Gluten-Free

This meal is jam-packed with flavour. It is like that of the traditional dish known as *stifado* (my other book has this recipe). The pickling onions (known as button or baby onion) release a fragrant and sweet flavor that marries perfectly well with the peppers and pork. This is great served with a bowl of plain rice or even some fried potatoes. Do not be tempted to add any water in the cooking process.

¾ cup olive oil

1 kg (2.2 lb. or 35.2 oz.) pork neck, cut into bite-size pieces

3 garlic cloves, quartered

7 baby onions, quartered

2 tablespoons red wine vinegar

450 g (0.99 lb. or 15.8 oz.) tomato puree

3 bay leaves

Salt and pepper to taste

2 teaspoons ground paprika

600 g (1.32 lb. or 21 oz.) red capsicums*

Heat the oil in a large skillet. Add the pork and cook on medium heat until browned on both sides. To this, add the garlic, onions, vinegar, puree, bay leaves, salt, pepper, and paprika. Do not add any water. Mix through all the ingredients, then lower heat, put a lid on the skillet, and allow it to simmer for approximately 1 hour, until the pork is fully cooked, juices have evaporated by half, and the olive oil has surfaced to the top.

While the pork is cooking, place the whole capsicums on a baking tray (unless using jarred*). Bake uncovered at 200°C (392°F) until soft and slightly blistered. Remove from the oven and place hot capsicums in a bowl covered with cling film. The steam will help soften the skins. After 15 minutes remove the cling film and gently peel off the skins and cut capsicums into rough quarters. Set aside in another bowl.

Once the pork is cooked, gently place the capsicums between the meat. Do not stir through. Cover and cook for another 15 minutes, then serve hot with a side salad, bowl of plain rice, or fried potatoes.

*Jarred bell peppers that are already baked can also be used. If so, use 500 g (1.1 lb. or 17.6 oz.) in this case, as the brine is usually quite vinegary.

Epiros

Τέταρτο 04

Epiros is geographically located in Northwestern Greece. It is amid the mountainous region called *Pindus*. This Pindus range is regularly termed "the spine of Greece" because it runs along the border of Thessaly and Epirus. It is a rugged terrain known for its farming products and prestigious vineyards. Though this region has a coast and faces the Ionian Sea, seafood is not primarily seen in the cuisine. Mountains are what stand out in this region, and thus what is eaten is chiefly shepherd's food. The region has ample pasture for grazing sheep, goats, wild boar, and deer and an extremely rich flora providing food for animals and bees . Herbs, and greens, are also scattered throughout the mountains, making for healthy pie fillings and used for medicinal treatments. A gastronomic hub for cheese-making and wine, some claim it to be the best in the country due to its landscape, height above sea-level, and alpine climate. Its highest mountain is Mount Smolikas, which has an altitude of 2,637 meters above sea level. Goats and sheep graze the mountains, which ultimately produce world-class exceptional milk, which then gets turned into butter and yogurt.

Classic meat dishes like *kleftiko*, meatballs in yogurt, and *kontosouvli* are some delicacies cooked in this region.

Olive trees do not overly produce and flourish on the mountainous regions of Epiros, and olives, therefore, are not used as a primary ingredient in their cuisine, but rather fresh butter. Flavors are reminiscent of the Balkans more than the remainder of Greece. Cheese-making has also long been a tradition in this region. Top-quality cheeses are also exported out of Epiros, such as *Dodoni feta*, smoked *metsovone*, *anthotiro* (salt-free cheese), a spicy hard *kefalotyri* cheese (made of goat's and sheep's milk), and *manouri*, another salt-free sheep's milk cheese. Due to these high-end products, the most famous foods are pies! Everything is made into a pie, with endless fillings, pie-type breads, and yogurt pastries. There are also some specialty desserts known in this region, such as *galatopita* (milk pie), *karidopita* (walnut pie), and *baklava* (syrup-drenched pastry with nuts). A common theme in these pies is the dairy component.

Mountains and Milk

Chocolate and Walnut Cake

Γιαννιώτικη Καρυδόπιτα

Serves 22 pieces
1 hour 10 minutes

Karidopita literally means *karidi*, "walnut," and *pita* for "pie." It is a syrup-drenched spiced walnut cake. Its flavors improve over time, so eating it the day after it is made is ideal. As far back as can be dated, the use of nuts and honey was dominant in the Greek cuisine. This cake, as with many recipes, has changed over time. It was originally a dense cake (due to not having raising agents at the time) and a very heavy honey syrup. It wasn't until the Byzantine era that sugars started to appear in households, where this cake also took a different form. Sugar was substituted for honey, and many versions were added and changed, such as adding liquor to the syrup, citrus zests, chocolate, butter to the eggs to help with rising, and semolina flour in exchange of bread crumbs. Though I am one for keeping recipes as original and authentic as possible, I could not see how a dense, heavy honey cake would be as appealing as this adaptation. My choice is semolina flour, a little dark chocolate to balance the sweetness, and sugar instead of honey. It is light, moist, and delicious!

7 whole eggs

150 g (0.33 lb. or 5.29 oz.) castor (superfine) sugar

30 g (0.06 lb. or 1.05 oz.) cocoa powder

½ teaspoon vanilla sugar

Pinch of salt

250 g (0.55 lb. or 8.81 oz.) coarse semolina flour

50 g (0.11 lb. or 1.76 oz.) all-purpose flour

2 teaspoons baking powder

2 teaspoons cinnamon powder

1 teaspoon clove powder

250 g (0.55 lb. or 8.81 oz.) crushed walnuts (not too fine), plus ½ cup for topping

120 g (0.26 lb. or 4.23 oz.) dark chocolate, chopped

Syrup:
500 mL (16.9 fl. oz.) water

1½ cups castor (superfine) sugar

Lemon peel, one slice

1 cinnamon quill

Preheat oven to 170°C (338°F).

Grease and line a baking dish (32 cm x 22 cm or 12.5 in. x 8.6 in.) with parchment paper. Set aside.

With an electric mixer, beat eggs with sugar until doubled in volume, thick, and pale in color (approximately 10 minutes). Combine the cocoa, vanilla sugar, salt, semolina, flour, baking powder, and spices with the egg mixture and beat until incorporated. Remove from mixer and add walnuts and chocolate, mixing with a wooden spoon and being careful not to overmix. Pour the cake batter into the baking dish and scatter the remaining walnuts over the top. Bake for 35–40 minutes or until a skewer inserted comes out clean. Allow to cool completely!

Now prepare the syrup. Add all ingredients into a small saucepan and bring to a boil. Simmer for 5 minutes, then pour hot syrup over the top of the cooled cake. It may seem as though it has a lot of syrup, but don't worry, it will be absorbed.

Allow the cake to sit (minimum 5 hours, or preferably overnight) in the refrigerator before serving. Cut and serve with a cup of coffee.

Milk Pie with Homemade Filo Pastry

Γαλατόπιτα με χωριάτικο φύλλο

Serves 12 pieces
1.5 hours

Galatopita can be made with or without pastry. It is a pie that dates to antiquity and uses few but staple ingredients that are usually found in one's pantry. *Gala* means "milk," and *pita* means "pie"! This recipe is with homemade pastry, though a store-bought pastry would also work. It is very simple to make and quick to prepare. It can be eaten both as a dessert or for breakfast. There are several flavor combinations that can be had, but vanilla in the custard and a good sprinkling of cinnamon powder to serve is most common. For extra flavor, I have added orange zest and walnuts!

Pastry:
2 cups all-purpose plain flour

2 tablespoons olive oil

1 tablespoon salt

1 teaspoon white or red wine vinegar

1 cup warm water

Corn flour (cornstarch) for rolling out filo pastry

½ cup olive oil for brushing pastry layers and top

Prepare filo pastry. Place all the ingredients into a large bowl. Bring together with a wooden spoon, then tip onto a floured benchtop and knead until soft and smooth. Add more flour, if needed, or water, if it is too dry. This should take a few minutes. Cover and rest for a minimum of 25 minutes.

In a bowl, add sugar, corn flour, semolina, and vanilla and mix well. Set aside.

Place milk in a pot and heat until hot but not boiling. Whisk in sugar and flour mixture until the milk has thickened and the mixture starts to boil. Remove from heat. Add zest and beaten eggs, vigorously whisking to combine. Do this quickly so the eggs do not scramble. Pour into a bowl and cover with cling film directly on the custard (this will eliminate a film forming on top). Set aside to cool as you prepare the sheets of pastry.

Oil a baking tray (35 cm or 13.7 in. diameter). Preheat oven to 190°C (374°F).

Divide dough into three pieces. Dust corn flour onto a workbench and place one piece of dough. Sprinkle corn flour on top. With a thin dowel, start to roll out pastry, dusting liberally with corn flour, to a circle a little larger than the baking tray. Place onto the baking tray, allowing edges to hang over the rim. Drizzle 2 tablespoons of oil over the pastry and sprinkle ½ tablespoon cinnamon powder, ½ tablespoon castor sugar, and walnuts (all walnuts in first layer). Repeat with three layers. Pour the filling and spread evenly. Fold in excess dough one layer at a time, drizzling with a little more olive oil so the pastry layers do not stick to each other.

Sprinkle castor sugar and cinnamon powder over the top and bake for 35–40 minutes or until the pastry is golden brown. Allow it to cool slightly, then sprinkle icing sugar and cinnamon powder. Serve warm or cold.

Tip: The filling can be made hours in advance and covered with cling film until needed.

Filling:

1 cup castor (superfine) sugar

100 g (0.22 lb. or 3.53 oz.) corn flour (cornstarch)

100 g (0.22 lb. or 3.53 oz.) semolina flour

½ a vanilla bean, deseeded

2 L (67.6 fl. oz.) whole milk

¼ orange, zested

2 whole eggs, lightly beaten

8 tablespoons olive oil, divided

2 tablespoons cinnamon powder, divided

2 tablespoons castor (superfine) sugar, divided

¾ cup walnuts, roasted and crushed

1 tablespoon icing (confectioners) sugar to sprinkle on top before serving

Milk Pie with Homemade Filo Pastry, page 113.

Sesame-Coated Feta Saganaki

Φέτα σαγανάκι

Serves 2
10 minutes
Gluten-Free

Greek cheese *saganaki* is fried cheese, with kefalograviera cheese being the most commonly used. In fact, the word *saganaki* comes from the Arabic word *sahn*, which is also the Turkish word sahan, which refers to the small copper dish with two handles that is used to fry the cheese. If you do not have this type of pan, any cast-iron skillet or fry pan will do. Traditionally, the cheese gets a splash of ouzo liquor, which is then lit upon serving to create a little theater and a wonderful taste. The recipe below does not call for any form of fire, on purpose, so that it is family friendly and a little simpler to prepare. This recipe is made with feta cheese instead of the more common yellow cheese. Use a hard Greek feta, not a creamy, soft variety. It will hold its shape better when frying. You can prepare the cheese in advance and keep covered in the refrigerator until you want to fry.

½ cup all-purpose flour (or rice flour for gluten-free alternative)

½ cup sesame seeds, toasted

1 whole egg, beaten

100 g (0.22 lb. or 3.5 oz.) block feta cheese

Olive oil to shallow fry

Juice of ½ lemon or 2 tablespoons runny honey or sour cherry spoon sweet* to serve

Take three small bowls. Place flour in one, sesame in another, and the beaten egg in the third bowl.

Take the block of feta and dip into the egg, shaking off any excess. Then dip into the flour, then egg, then into flour again, then the sesame seeds. Coat evenly. Set aside in the refrigerator for a minimum of 10 minutes.

Heat oil (roughly ½ cup) in a small frying pan on medium heat. Place cheese in the pan and cook until golden on both sides. Place on a paper towel to drain any excess oil. To serve, squeeze half a lemon or drizzle warm honey or spoon sweet. Serve warm as an entree.

*Sour cherry spoon sweets are available from Mediterranean grocers.
Tip: You can slice the feta into a thinner piece if you prefer.

Baklava with shredded pastry, page 121.

Facts About Baklava

Many scholars have suggested that the origins of baklava date back to 160 BC, from an ancient Roman dish called *placenta*, a dish consisting of many layers of dough, filled with a mixture of cheese, spiced with bay leaves, and drenched in honey. Cato, a Roman historian, documented this recipe and writes in his *De Agri Cultura* (160 BC):

> Shape the placenta as follows: place a single row of tracta along the whole length of the base dough. This is then covered with the mixture [cheese and honey] from the mortar. Place another row of tracta on top and go on doing so until all the cheese and honey have been used up. Finish with a layer of tracta…place the placenta in the oven and put a preheated lid on top of it…When ready, honey is poured over the placenta.

Plakous or *plakountos* is derived from the Greek word for "thin" or "layered." This same word was also adapted by the Armenians, describing any dessert made of honey and bread. From Armenia, it then appeared in Arabic cookbooks due to the Cilician Armenians, who settled in Asia Minor, Northern Syria, and Turkey. No doubt this Roman dessert evolved itself over time through the Byzantine Empire to our modern baklava. One thing has remained constant: the preparation of handmade, thin sheets of flaky, buttery pastry. Many evidences throughout this century suggest that sheets of pastry, *yufka* (as known in Turkey), or *filo* (as known in Greece), were used and then filled with various mixtures.

Baklava with Shredded Pastry

Γιαννιώτικος μπακλαβάς

Serves 36 pieces
1.5 hours
plus 5 hours refrigeration

The Greek island Lesvos still serves a dessert called *platcenta* (πλατσεντα) — a baklava filled with nuts (rather than the original cheese) and drenched in honey. It is a delicately acquired skill to make this thin pastry, which was perfected by skilled cooks and typically served to those in high society. These days, ready-made filo pastry is a great substitute. So in talking about baklava, we arrive at the *gianiotiko baklava* — yet again similar but slightly different. It consists of spiced nuts and shredded pastry, drizzled with butter, all rolled together into the shape of a cigar, then topped with extra butter and drenched with a sweet sugar syrup. From its origins to its evolved state of what we have today, any form of baklava will have you salivating!

12 sheets filo pastry, store-bought

175 g (0.38 lb. or 6.17 oz.) kataifi pastry*

Whole cloves for garnish

Pistachios, crushed, for garnish

Sugar syrup:
2 cups castor (superfine) sugar

2 cups water

2 tablespoons glucose syrup

½ a lemon, juiced

5 whole cloves

Preheat oven to 160°C (320°F).

Place all the ingredients for the sugar syrup into a saucepan. Bring to a boil, then simmer for 8 minutes. Remove from heat and allow it to cool completely. Set aside.

Place all the ingredients for the filling into a bowl and mix to combine. Set aside.

Butter a baking tray 32 cm x 25 cm (12.5 in. x 9.8 in.). Remove kataifi pastry from the packet and gently pull the strands apart so there are no clumps. Divide into 6 bundles. Set aside.

To assemble: Take one piece of filo pastry and lay it flat onto workbench. Drizzle some melted butter over the pastry. Place another sheet on top. Take one bundle of kataifi and spread over the pastry. Take a handful of the filling mixture and spread over the top.

Place a thin dowel or two skewers in the center. Gently lift the filo closest to you and place over the skewers, covering the filo so that it is folded in half. Carefully roll into a cylinder, having the skewers in the center. Once it is rolled up, place both hands on the end of the pastry, holding onto the skewers that are exposed on the ends. Gently gather pastry, pushing into the center, then remove the skewers. Gently place onto baking tray with seam side down, snuggling each log close together.

Repeat with another 5 rolls. With a sharp knife, being careful not to cut all the way down, score the desired shape and pour the remaining butter over the top.

Bake for 40–50 minutes or until golden. Once removed from the oven, pour over the cold syrup. Allow it to absorb the syrup before eating, approximately 5 hours. Place a whole clove and scatter crushed pistachios over the top of each piece for garnish. Store uncovered (so the filo retains its crunch) in the refrigerator for up to two days.

*Kataifi pastry is sold at Mediterranean grocers.

Filling:
100 g (0.22 lb. or 3.52 oz.) almonds, roasted, and crushed

150 g (0.33 lb. or 5.29 oz.) walnuts, crushed

2 tablespoons cinnamon powder

½ teaspoon clove powder

¼ cup castor (superfine) sugar

For Drizzling:
250 g (0.55 lb. or 8.81 oz.) butter, melted

Yogurt and Cheese Pie

Ηπειρώτικη Αλευρόπιτα

Serves 21 pieces
1 hour

This pie marks the region of Epiros. It is a versatile, quick recipe to prepare with the simplest ingredients on hand. Also known by names such as *zimaropita* (Dough Pie), *tis stigmis* (This-Minute Pie), *zarkopita* (zarkos meaning "naked"), or *kasiopita* (kasiou meaning "cheese" in this region's dialect). Some use milk, others use yogurt or both, but whichever choice, the main ingredient must be a good-quality feta cheese. This pie must be thin and baked till crispy around the edges and golden in the middle. Essentially, this pie is made from a pancake batter consistency that is poured into a hot pan that has been oiled. You must ensure the batter is not thick and that the pan is steaming hot before pouring the mixture into the tray. The oil creates a beautiful crust under the pie. This is best eaten hot or warm!

90 mL (3.04 fl. oz.) olive oil

250 g (0.55 lb. or 8.81 oz.) all-purpose plain flour

1 cup whole milk, warmed

½ tablespoon dried oregano

140 g (0.3 lb. or 4.9 oz.) yogurt

2 whole eggs

Salt and pepper to taste

500 g (1.1 lb. or 17.6 oz.) feta cheese, crumbled and divided

1 tablespoon black sesame (optional)

1 tablespoon raw sesame

Preheat oven to 180°C (356°F).

Pour the olive oil into a baking tray measuring 30 cm x 23 cm (11 in. x 9 in.). Place in the oven and allow it to heat up until the mixture below is ready.

In a bowl, place all the ingredients except the feta cheese and sesame seeds. Whisk to combine well, ensuring all lumps have been removed. The batter should not be thick (otherwise the result will be rubbery) but should drop from a spoon like a pancake batter. Add a little more milk to loosen (if needed). Add half the crumbled feta cheese and mix to combine.

Remove the baking tray from the oven and carefully pour the batter over the hot oil. Spread out evenly over the base of the pan. Scatter the remaining feta cheese over the batter and then sprinkle the sesame seeds over the top. Bake for 30 minutes or until golden. Remove from oven and allow it to cool slightly before slicing.

Tip: Traditionally, caramelized sliced onions are layered on the bottom of the tray with the oil, then the batter gets poured over the top and baked.

Spiced Meatballs in a Lemon Yogurt Sauce

Κεφτεδάκια με γιαούρτι

Serves 4
45 minutes

These aromatic meatballs are exceptionally delicious. They are rolled up into small, walnut-size balls, then dressed with a yogurt lemon sauce, which adds a great bite of freshness. They are easy to prepare and showcase the wonderful combination of meat and yogurt.

Meatballs:
500 g (1.1 lb. or 17.6 oz.) beef, minced

½ cup bread crumbs

1 large onion, chopped

2 tablespoons mint, finely chopped

1 whole egg, lightly beaten

½ cup olive oil, divided

Salt and pepper to taste

1 teaspoon cumin powder

Sauce:
1 cup water

1 tablespoon cornstarch (diluted in 2 tablespoons water)

1 cup yogurt

1 lemon, juiced

Salt to taste

In a bowl, place the beef, bread crumbs, onion, mint, egg, ¼ cup olive oil, salt, pepper, and cumin powder and knead with your hands to combine well. Set aside for 10 minutes. Now take a teaspoon of the mince and roll with your palms to create small balls (approximately 34 pieces). Place on a plate until they are all done.

Take a wide saucepan and add remaining ¼ cup olive oil. Heat well and add the meatballs. Allow them to cook, turning on all sides. This should take around 10 minutes. Remove meatballs and set aside to proceed with the yogurt sauce.

Pour one cup of water into the same saucepan, and with a wooden spoon, scrape off any bits of meat that have stuck to the pan (called deglazing). Add the cornstarch (which has been diluted with 2 tablespoons water), and whisk to remove any lumps. Remove from the heat and add the yogurt, lemon juice, and salt, mixing to incorporate well. Place onto the burner again and slightly heat through, ensuring the yogurt does not boil. Taste and adjust the seasoning. It should have a salty lemon tang. Serve immediately onto a platter, together with lemon wedges and a dusting of paprika powder.

Cheese Pie with Shredded Pastry

Τυρόπιτα με φύλλο κανταΐφι

Serves 15 pieces
2 hours
(and/or optional 11 hours overnight soaking - see introduction)

This pie is preferably prepared the day before you want it baked. The juices get soaked up by the pastry to create a super moist pie. If you do not have the luxury of time, you could prepare the pie and allow it to sit for 30 minutes before baking. The smell of the cheeses melting away and the pastry going golden while this pie cooks gets your mouth salivating. This cheese pie showcases the amazing produce of this region. Dairy at its finest, this pie is full of flavor! Don't deprive yourself of the best milk, eggs, and cheeses you can find, and avoid low-fat products at all costs! Eat full fat, but just eat less of it. This recipe is made up of few ingredients, but of greatest quality. Shredded pastry gives a delicious crunch to the pie. It is best eaten the day it is baked, otherwise the top goes soft.

¼ cup olive oil, divided

375 g (0.82 lb. or 13.2 oz.) kataifi pastry*

500 g (1.1 lb. or 17.6 oz.) ricotta cheese, crumbled

200 g (0.44 lb. or 7.05 oz.) feta cheese, crumbled

60 g (0.13 lb. or 2.1 oz.) kefalograviera cheese, grated*

500 mL (16.9 fl. oz.) whole milk

3 whole eggs, beaten

¼ teaspoon ground nutmeg

Salt and pepper to taste

½ cup toasted sesame seeds to garnish (optional)

*Kataifi pastry and kefalograviera cheese can be purchased at European grocers. Kefalograviera cheese can be substituted with Parmesan cheese.

Remove the kataifi from the packet and pull apart with your hands to remove any lumps. The pastry should be light, fluffy, and doubled in volume. Set aside. Pour 2 tablespoons of oil into a baking tray (30 cm x 20 cm x 6 cm or 11.8 in. x 7.8 in. x 2.3 in.). Place half the shredded pastry, covering the base of the tray. Pat down slightly with your hands. Set aside.

In a bowl, combine the ricotta, feta, and kefalograviera cheese. Mix with a fork to combine well. Place this mixture on top of the shredded pastry in the baking tray. It will be thick, so drop spoonfuls, then level with a fork to cover the pastry. Take the remaining pastry and cover the top. Lightly press down on the top to create an even layer. Take the milk and eggs together with the nutmeg, salt, and pepper and mix in a bowl. With a ladle, pour over the pie, ensuring the top is totally covered. Pour the remaining olive oil over the top. Allow the pie to stand overnight in the fridge, covered with foil. The next day remove from fridge, preheat oven to 170°C (338°F), and bake for 30–40 minutes or until golden on the top and bottom. Allow to cool slightly. Serve warm with scattered toasted sesame seeds (for an optional crunch).

Slow-Cooked Lamb and Potatoes in Baking Paper

Αρνί κλέφτικο στη λαδόκολλα

Serves 3-4
4-5 hours
Gluten-Free

Cooking methods have varied over time and in different cultures. Ancient Greeks cooked many meals outdoors over open coals or in brick, outdoor woodfire ovens prior to our usage of domestic conventional ovens. This dish has derived from this ancient method. *Kleftiko* literally means "stolen" (in this case, lamb), which dates back to ancient times. It is said that thieving Greek robbers would dig a deep pit in the ground and place wood and coals until the fire became a smolder. They would then place the stolen lamb on top and cover it with vegetation to add moisture and allow it to cook for hours underground. These days, Greeks rarely use "earth ovens," so an adaptation which has emerged is the wrapping of parchment paper to encase the meat, resulting in a slow-cooked, juicy one-pot meal. This meal is cooked low and slow until it is falling off the bone!

1 kg (2.2 lb. or 35.27 oz.) lamb shoulder or leg

3 large potatoes, quartered

2 tablespoons dried or fresh rosemary

1 tablespoon dried oregano

½ cup olive oil

4 garlic cloves, halved

½ cup lemon juice

Salt and pepper to taste

1 cup water

Preheat oven to 160°C (320°F).

Place parchment paper onto a baking tray large enough to be able to close. Place all the ingredients onto the parchment paper, mixing to combine well. Fold over the paper to enclose. Place a layer of aluminum foil over the top to seal or place the package in a Dutch oven with a lid for maximum heat.

Bake for 4 hours. Open the package and cook for a further 30 minutes or until the lamb and potatoes are golden. Place the baking tray immediately at the table, served directly from the package. Serve with a Greek salad and tzatziki sauce.

Olive Oil Spiced Pie

Λαδόπιτα

Serves 20 pieces. 1 hour 15 minutes
Gluten-Free, Dairy-Free, Egg-Free

I find anything that is associated with the olive tree tremendously charming. From the fascinating wood, both in texture and color, to the liquid gold that is excreted from the olive! In this recipe, the star is the olive oil. It is heavy and prominent in taste, and the texture therefore is best when eaten the day after it is made. There are two variations of an olive oil slice; one is super soft, and the other is slightly crunchy on the exterior. This recipe is the latter. It has a wonderful gingerbread flavor and a consistency comparable to a gooey brownie. The aroma is reminiscent of Christmas due to the cinnamon and clove. Truth be told, I had avoided trying this, even though I had seen it countless times in books and on our trips to Greece. It looked somewhat bland, and therefore I didn't care for it. However, on my most recent trip to Greece, while I was gazing in the window of a Greek bakery, I was approached by the owner of the shop. She asked if I wanted to buy some, and immediately I said, no, thank you! Very convincingly, she persuaded me that I should try it at least once. She continued to tell me that this once would have me going back for more! She was right. I hesitantly ate some, then went in for a second bite, until I ate the whole piece. The next day I wanted another slice, so back I went to buy some more. All this to say, this is worth making and tastes rather unusual in a pleasant way. Use the best olive oil you can source. Serve with a cup of strong coffee or tea.

1 cup castor (superfine) sugar

1 cup water

1 cup olive oil

½ cup orange juice, freshly squeezed

1 lemon, zested

½ cup runny honey

1 tablespoon cinnamon powder

¼ teaspoon clove powder

250 g (0.55 lb. or 8.81 oz.) all-purpose flour

250 g (0.55 lb. or 8.81 oz.) semolina flour

4 tablespoons sesame seeds, raw

Cinnamon powder to serve

On medium heat, place sugar, water, and oil into a medium stove pot and bring to a boil or heat until sugar has melted. To this, add the orange juice, zest, honey, cinnamon, and clove. Mix to incorporate, and the honey melts. Add the flour and semolina a little at a time, stirring continuously until it becomes thick and starts to pull away from the sides of the pot. This should take about 6–7 minutes. Keep stirring for an additional 3–4 minutes so that all the moisture has been dried out. Remove from the stove.

Preheat oven to 180°C (356°F). Take a baking pan (24 cm or 9.44 in. square) and sprinkle 2 tablespoons sesame seeds on the bottom. Pour in the mixture and flatten with a wooden spoon. Take a fork and, using the handle, carefully score the cake into slices, wetting the handle if it gets sticky. Scatter another 2 tablespoons sesame seeds over the top. Bake for approximately 50 minutes or until golden. Allow to cool completely, then serve with a sprinkling of cinnamon powder. It can be stored for up to a week in a sealed container. It does not need refrigeration. It is best eaten the day after it is made.

Olive Oil Spiced Pie, page 130.

Crete is the largest island in Greece, located 400 miles northwest of Alexandria, Egypt. Alongside its wonderful cuisine, Crete has exquisite mountains, the highest of which is 2,500 meters, located south of Rethymno, with impressive cliffs and a breathtaking abundance of beaches. Minoan civilization (also known as the Bronze Age Civilization from 2,000 BC) is possibly the major reason Crete is recognized. *Minos* is the dynastic name given to a ruler of Crete. Crete was the first center of high civilization of the Aegean Sea before extending to neighboring islands and then to the mainland. They were famous for the palaces they built, such as Knossos, and their art, architecture, and pottery. Minoan culture and trade influenced the Aegean through interaction with Crete. The textiles and pottery were a symbol of prestige that spread rapidly in the Eastern Mediterranean. The decline of the Minoan civilization and end was around 1100 BC. Speculations attribute this to the volcanic eruption in Santorini, which damaged trade routes (although Crete was not directly affected by the eruption). So there was Roman (AD 67–824), Arab (AD 824–961) Byzantine (AD 961–1204), Venetian (AD 1204–1669), and Turkish (AD 1669–1913), occupation. Crete was independent until AD 1913, when it was united to Greece. So many cultures passed through the island, yet the Cretans preserved their culinary traditions.

Crete is recognized for the production of high-quality extra-virgin olive oil (the secret to longevity for the Cretan people), vineyards for winemaking, agriculture, a botanical bliss of herbs, cheese-making, and cattle-breeding. The making and drinking of a strong distilled Cretan spirit called raki (*tsikoudia*), or otherwise known as Cretan nectar, is also an island staple. It is made from the distillation of the skins and pits left over from pressing grapes. The alcohol content is usually around 37 percent. Most Cretans make their own home brew and consume it daily. They say a glass of raki is a glass of friendship and Cretan hospitality. One is greeted into a home with a chilled glass of raki, also ending a meal with it, amid many more throughout the evening.

Wild herbs and greens grow along the hillsides of Cretan mountains and cliffs. Gathered by the woman of the household, these greens get blanched and drizzled with an olive oil and lemon dressing, sautéed for pies, or even boiled and drunk as a tea. Medicinal treatments come first by the aid of these herbs. Produce is picked and eaten seasonally, with very little spices and sauces added to the cooking process. Foods are prepared simply, retaining their nutritional value. Freshness from the wild greens and fragrance from the aromatic herbs and flowers are the dishes of Crete. Herbal teas consumed with local honey are drunk and used for medicinal properties. It is fair to say, just eat like a Cretan, and you will be eating nutritional, beneficial food that ensures a well-balanced, healthy lifestyle!

Rugged Beauty

Vanilla Pastries

Καλιτσούνια λυχναράκια

Serves 20 pieces
1 hour

Kalitsounia can be made with a savory filling of wild greens, a salty cheese or with a sweet filling made with sweetened cheese and cinnamon and drizzled with honey. They can be shaped as a parcel or an oil lamp, can be fried or baked, and can be made with filo pastry or a thick yogurt pastry. These ones are called *kalitsounia lihnarakia*. These are the sweetened version. Cretans use a local cheese called *tiromalama*, but a ricotta or mascarpone cheese also works well. Double the batch and freeze. Then remove from the freezer, thaw, and bake. Though slightly sweetened, they can be eaten as an appetizer.

Pastry:
¼ cup olive oil

¼ teaspoon baking powder

1 whole egg, lightly whisked

¼ teaspoon vanilla sugar

½ cup castor (superfine) sugar

¼ cup whole milk

320 g (0.7 lb. or 11.2 oz.) all-purpose flour, plus a little more

Filling:
400 g (0.88 lb. or 11.28 oz.) ricotta cheese

3 tablespoons castor (superfine) sugar

¼ teaspoon vanilla sugar or 1 vanilla bean

To finish:
1 whole egg to brush over top

Cinnamon to dust

Honey to serve

Preheat oven to 150°C (302°F).

In a bowl, place the oil, baking powder, egg, vanilla sugar, castor sugar, and milk. Whisk to combine, then, using a wooden spoon, add flour ½ cup at a time until a dough comes together. Place onto a floured board and knead until a soft and pliable dough is formed. Add a little more flour if need be. Cover and allow to rest until the filling is prepared.

Prepare the filling by placing the ricotta cheese into a bowl. Break it up with a fork, then add sugar and vanilla. Mix to incorporate and remove any lumps from the cheese.

Halve the dough, setting one half aside. Place remaining dough between two pieces of parchment paper. Using a rolling pin, flatten dough to 0.5 cm (0.19 in.) thickness. With a cookie cutter (6 cm or 2.3 in.), cut rounds. Place one round into your palm and add one teaspoon of filling into the center. Pinch the ends to create the shape. Place onto a baking tray. Brush egg wash and sprinkle cinnamon powder. Bake for 15–20 minutes or until golden. Serve with honey or an extra sprinkling of cinnamon powder. These are best eaten on the day they are made. Do not cover, otherwise the pastry will go soft.

Fried Snails with Rosemary

Χοχλιοί μπουρμπουριστοί με δεντρολίβανο

Serves 4
1.5 hours
Gluten-Free*

Cretan food is never complex but can be a little strange. Eating snails is not what you would commonly see on a menu, that is, if you are outside of Crete. Cretans have a reputation of serving up some of the best fried snails in Greece and beyond. They accompany these appetizers with raki, a Cretan brandy made from distilled grapes. After any rains, the Cretan women go to collect these fresh morsels that start to expose themselves from under and beneath greenery. They are plump and very tasty.

1 kg (2.2 lb. or 35.27 oz.) snails, membranes removed and cleaned

2 cups white wine

2 bay leaves

3 garlic cloves, whole

Salt to taste

½ cup all-purpose flour*

½ cup olive oil

2 tablespoons chopped rosemary

½ cup red wine vinegar

Place the snails in a saucepan with wine and enough water to cover them. Add bay leaves and garlic and simmer on low heat for 30 minutes, removing any scum that forms on the top. Set aside to cool in the saucepan.

Heat oil in a frying pan.

Drain the snails and add some salt. Add flour to the snails, shaking off any excess flour. Place into the hot oil, with the shell opening facing down, and fry for 2–3 minutes. Do not mix. Add the rosemary and vinegar and allow to cook for a further 3 minutes or until vinegar has evaporated. Sprinkle a little more salt and serve immediately.

*For gluten-free, use cornstarch instead of flour.

Ricotta Pancakes with Honey

Σφακιανές πίτες

Serves 12 flatbreads
40 minutes

These pies get their name from the mountainous region of *Sfakia* in southern Crete. They resemble a pancake but are slightly thicker, have a distinct aniseed flavor from the liquor, and are stuffed with ricotta cheese (otherwise known as mizithra cheese). Boasting some of Cretans' best produce, they consist of olive oil, raki (brandy), and local Cretan cheese, served with local honey. These pies can be served as an appetizer, a dessert, and even a breakfast meal. If you can't source Cretan cheese, a fresh ricotta will also work well. Certainly, use Greek Attica or Cretan honey for maximum authentic taste.

240 mL (8.11 fl. oz.) water (this is approximate; depending on your flour, you may need a little more or less)

2 tablespoons olive oil

1½ teaspoons salt

100 mL (3.38 fl. oz.) ouzo or raki*

3–4 cups all-purpose flour

400 g (0.88 lb. or 14.1 oz.) ricotta cheese, crumbled

Olive oil for frying

Lukewarm runny honey (heated in a pot) to serve

½ cup sesame seeds, toasted, to serve

Cinnamon powder to serve

*Raki can be purchased from European liquor stores or can be substituted with ouzo liquor.

In a bowl, add the water, oil, salt, and liquor. Slowly add spoonfuls of flour, mixing with a wooden spoon until a soft dough is formed. It must not be too sticky or too dry. When the dough has come together, move the dough to a lightly floured board or bench and knead it well for approximately 8 minutes. The dough should be soft and smooth. Cover it and allow it to rest for 10 minutes.

Crumble the ricotta cheese into a bowl. Take 1 tablespoon and roll into a ball with your hands. Do 12 balls and set aside.

To form the flatbread, divide the dough into 12 pieces. Take a piece and roll it into a ball using your palms or using a circular motion on your bench. Then, using your fingers, push the dough out from the center to create a crater in the middle to fill with cheese. Take a ball of cheese and place it into the dough pocket. Bring the sides of dough together to enclose the cheese inside. Flatten the dough with your palm, and then, on a floured bench, gently push down with a rolling pin. Slowly roll the dough into a circle approximately 10 cm (3.9 in.) in diameter and 1 cm (0.4 in.) in thickness.

In a pan, heat 3–4 tablespoons of olive oil. Once it is hot, add one flatbread at a time, cooking it until it becomes golden brown. Repeat this process on the opposite side. It should take no more than 1–2 minutes on each side. Repeat this process until all the flatbreads are cooked. Serve drizzled with lukewarm honey, scattered with sesame seeds, and dusted with cinnamon powder.

Dakos Salad

Ντάκος σαλάτα

Serves 4
15 minutes

To do a chapter on Crete and not include some form of a *dako* is like cooking a Greek meal and omitting olive oil. It is so commonly eaten and so easily prepared. Dakos is a rusk made of whole-grain barley flour, water, and salt. It is made into small rolls that are then baked and dried in the oven, intensifying the nutty flavor of the bread. Once dried, it hardens and needs to be run under water to soften. It is topped with grated tomatoes (which seep into the rusk), crumbled feta cheese, dried oregano, and olives and drizzled with a generous helping of olive oil. Alternatively, it can be crushed into bite-size pieces and added to a salad, as this recipe suggests. Dried rusks were developed many centuries ago as a means of keeping bread preserved for a long time. The name is predicted to have come from a Byzantine baker by the name of Paxamos, hence the Greek name *paximadi*, used for "dried rusks."

2 large dakos (Barley rusks)*

4 ripe tomatoes, chopped into bite-size pieces

1 tomato, grated

100 g (0.22 lb. or 3.52 oz.) feta cheese, crumbled

¼ cup Kalamata olives

½ cup olive oil

1 tablespoon parsley, chopped

1 tablespoon capers

Salt to taste

1 tablespoon dried oregano

1 tablespoon balsamic vinegar (optional)

Run the dakos under cold water for 1 minute. Crush slightly into bite-size pieces and place in a salad bowl. Add all the remaining ingredients and mix well to combine. Allow it to sit for 10 minutes before serving to allow the juices to permeate the dakos. Serve as a side.

*Barley rusks are readily available at Mediterranean grocers.

Cretan teas are exceptionally therapeutic in their benefits and delicious in taste! In addition to the common chamomile, fennel, bay leaf, thyme, and mint teas widely known around Greece, Crete also has a plethora of other herbs that are made into teas and drunk and consumed both cold and hot. Most herbs are grown on the mountainous regions of the island, where they are collected, dried, and stored. All teas can be made using fresh or dried herbs. Fresh herbs are lighter in taste and color, whereas dried herbs produce a darker and slightly stronger tea. Dried teas tend to also be richer in vitamins and minerals. All teas below are made with dried herbs. *Please note that I am not a physician and therefore do not propose this information to substitute any medical treatment, diagnosis, or therapy.*

Mountain Tea (otherwise known as *Malotira*, *Sideritis* [ironwort], or *tsai tou vounou*)
This is the most characteristic of the Cretan herbs. It is collected in July during the flowering season. This tea aids to fight colds, is used as a diuretic, and helps calm the stomach. It has high levels of antioxidants, essential oils, flavonoids, and phytonutrients.
To make 2 cups of Mountain tea: Fill a tea pot with 2 cups of water. Bring to a boil. Add one handful of dried mountain tea. Cover and boil for one minute, then turn stove off and allow the herbs to steep for another 3 minutes. Pour the tea through a strainer and serve with a teaspoon (per cup) of raw Greek honey.
Tip: For additional flavor, add one cinnamon stick to the water before boiling. Remove before serving. For a cold tea, add ice cubes and a slice of lemon.

***Faskomilo* Tea (otherwise known as Sage Tea)**
Faskomilo is the herb that feels a little like soft velvet. It is a beautiful green color when picked fresh but darkens when dried. It is commonly drunk to relieve menopause-related ailments and purifies blood, stomach, and bowel function. It is also used to treat ulcers, tonsilitis, and the like. High in antioxidants and levels of vitamin K, which is good for bone health, sage tea helps aid in memory loss and depression symptoms.
Prepare according to the Mountain Tea directions above. Ensure you do not steep for longer than 3 minutes, as the sage can become bitter. Strain and serve with a teaspoon (per cup) of raw Greek honey.

***Rigani* or Wild Oregano Tea**
Yes, the final touch to a Greek salad—wild dried oregano—is far more beneficial than you know and can be made into a tea! Named "joy of the mountain" from *origanon*, referring to *oros*, "mountain," and the verb *ganousthai*, meaning "to delight in." Those who have tried it know well that not many other types of oregano come close to the potency, flavor, and smell. Used as an antiseptic and a medicine for tooth- and stomachaches, wild oregano is a staple in both foods and drink and is also high in vitamin C and iron.
Prepare according to the Mountain Tea directions above, but infuse for 5 minutes. Strain and serve without any sweetener.

***Dentrolivano* or Rosemary Tea**
It is said this is the pick-me-up for headaches and migraines and helps digestion. An antiseptic and antibacterial, it is frequently used for hair loss of the scalp.
Prepare according to the Mountain Tea directions above, but infuse for 5 minutes. Strain and serve without any sweetener.

Stewed Chicken with Sage and Rosemary

Κοτόπουλο με φασκόμηλο και δεντρολίβανο

Serves 4
1 hour
Gluten-Free

Rosemary and sage work wonderfully well with chicken. Once again, the prominent use of herbs and the simplicity of a one-pot meal sums up the Cretan way. This dish is uncomplicated and yet delicious. Use organic chicken if available and, ideally, fresh herbs.

½ cup olive oil

2 onions, thinly sliced

2 tablespoons fresh rosemary, chopped

5 large sage leaves, chopped

Salt and pepper to taste

1 whole chicken, cut into portions

1 cup white wine

2 cups water

1 teaspoon tomato paste

1 lemon, juiced

Heat oil in a saucepan on medium heat. Add onions, rosemary, and sage, sautéing until soft and translucent. Season chicken and add to the pan. Brown on both sides. Add wine and cook for 3 minutes, then add water. Cover and cook for approximately 25 minutes or until the chicken is cooked through.

In a small bowl, dilute the tomato paste with the lemon juice. Pour over chicken and cook for a further 10–20 minutes or until juices have evaporated by half. Serve immediately with plain rice or fried potatoes.

Chicken with Mandarin, Orange, Honey and Thyme

Ψητό κοτόπουλο με μανταρίνι, πορτοκαλί, μέλι και θυμάρι

Serves 4
2 hours
Gluten-Free

Crete has an abundance of herbs, honey, and olive oil that, when combined, can develop into the most wonderful, hearty meal. Everyone has their own take on a roast chicken dinner, but this Cretan specialty surely tops the list. Strong citrus flavors of mandarin, orange, and lemon permeate the dish. The juices, together with honey, garlic, dried oregano, thyme, and olive oil, are poured over the bird and potatoes, then roasted until crisp. Not much else but a simple salad and a glass of Cretan wine is needed to complete this dish. Always ensure you use Greek dried oregano and the best-quality honey you can find.

2 mandarins, juiced

1 orange, juiced (reserving the skin)

1 lemon, juiced (reserving the skin)

2 garlic cloves, crushed

¾ cup olive oil

¼ cup runny honey

Salt and pepper to taste

1 tablespoon dried oregano

1½ cups water

1 whole chicken

1.3 kg (2.86 lb. or 45.85 oz.) potatoes, washed and quartered

6 thyme stalks

Preheat oven to 200°C (392°F).

To a bowl, add the juices of the mandarins, orange, and lemon (reserving the skins). Add the crushed garlic, oil, honey, salt, pepper, oregano, and water. Whisk to combine well. Taste it. It should have a sweet and a little overseasoned taste at this stage. Adjust seasoning if needed. Set aside.

Place chicken in a baking tray, placing potatoes around it. Stuff the chicken cavity with the reserved lemon and orange skin and half the thyme. Pour the juice mixture over the chicken and potatoes. Sprinkle a little more salt over the chicken and scatter the remaining thyme leaves over the top.

Bake for 1–2 hours or until chicken and potatoes are golden and cooked and juices have evaporated by half. Serve immediately with a Greek salad.

Wild Weeds with Lemon and Olive Oil

Χόρτα

Serves 4
25 minutes
Gluten-Free

At the heart of Cretan cooking (and a staple throughout Greece) is a plate of greens, so unpretentious and yet delightful. Olive oil is drizzled over the top in no fancy way, and a squeeze of lemon juice is added for freshness and tang. During the hot summer months, these wild greens grow in overabundance. Perceived as weeds to the non-Greek, these wild greens are edible weeds that are therapeutic and appetizing. Add to any meze table, and these greens are gone in a flash. Though we don't have the accessibility to eat the exact greens from Crete, there are many other varieties that can be used, such as spinach, dandelions, chicory, chard, silver beets, beetroot leaves, stinging nettle, and so on. The amaranth (vlita in Greek) are widely available and are a sweeter green to use in this recipe. Do not be astounded at the amount of greens used in this recipe. Once boiled, the greens shrink and the volume is decreased incredibly.

1.5 kg (3.3 lb. or 52.91 oz.) amaranth (or other leafy greens), washed and cut in half

¼ cup olive oil

Lemon juice to taste

Salt to taste

Fill a large pot with water and a tablespoon of salt (to fit at least 4 liters). Bring to a boil, then place half the greens. Allow them to cook for around 10 minutes or until softened. Remove and place in a colander to drain excess water. Repeat with remaining greens.

Place drained greens onto a serving platter, sprinkle extra salt (if desired), drizzle olive oil over the top, and add lemon juice. Gently mix together and serve cold or at room temperature. Adjust seasoning to your taste.

This can be served as an appetizer or as a side dish with seafood.

Cookies with Mahlepi, Mastiha, and Orange

Κουλουράκια με μαχλέπι, μαστίχα και πορτοκάλι

Serves 75 pieces
1.5 hours

Koulourakia is plural for "small biscuit." These biscuits are slightly sweet and aromatic, with flavors of *tsoureki* (a bread baked at Easter time; the recipe is in my cookbook, *Hellenic Kanella*). As you bite into the softish center and slightly crunchy biscuit, you get a slight bitter undertone from the orange rind and the prominent flavors of mastiha and mahlepi.* Always ensure the butter and sugar are well beaten until a white, creamy texture is achieved. This will ensure a fluffy texture. Once removed from the oven, they may seem soft, but they will harden once they cool.

1 orange rind (carefully removed with peeler, omitting the white pith)

3 tablespoons castor (superfine) sugar

100 mL (3.38 fl. oz.) orange juice, freshly squeezed

1 teaspoon baking powder

1 teaspoon baking soda

200 g (0.44 lb. or 7.05 oz.) butter, room temperature

1½ cups castor (superfine) sugar, divided

3 whole eggs

2 teaspoons mahlepi powder*

1 teaspoon crushed mastiha*

900 g (1.98 lb. or 31.7 oz.) plain white flour

1 tablespoon whole milk

1 egg yolk

*Mastiha resin and mahlepi powder can be purchased from Mediterranean grocers.

Preheat oven to 180°C (365°F). Place the orange rind, 3 tablespoons sugar, and enough water to cover in a pan. Simmer on a low heat for 20–30 minutes or until the bitterness from the orange isn't as stringent. Discard liquid, then chop up the rind as small as possible. Set aside.

Combine the orange juice, baking powder, and baking soda in a bowl and mix. It will fizzle slightly. Set aside. In a stand mixer, mix the butter and sugar and cream together until white and fluffy (around 10 minutes). Incorporate the 3 eggs (beating one egg at a time). Add the cooked orange rind, mahlepi, mastiha, and orange juice mixture. Mix well. At this point it may look as though it has curdled—don't worry, it will be fine once the flour is added.

Remove whisk and use the paddle attachment. Slowly add spoonfuls of flour and mix to combine. Keep adding flour until you have a pliable and soft dough. It must not be sticky to the hands. If so, keep adding a little more flour. Remove from mixer and place on a lightly floured bench. Allow to rest for 20 minutes, covered with a clean tea towel.

Take a handful of dough and start to roll out into long cords, length 17 cm (6.7 in.), weighing 20 grams (0.7 oz.). Twist together to create the traditional shape (alternatively, you can make snail-like shapes). In a small bowl, combine the milk with the egg yolk. Mix together and brush over koulourakia with a pastry brush. Place on a baking tray lined with parchment paper. Bake for 25–30 minutes or until golden brown. Cool completely and store in an airtight container for up to 3 weeks.

Aegean Islands

Έκτο 06

The Aegean Islands can be grouped three ways: Dodecanese, Cyclades, and North Aegean. They have been influenced by the surrounding countries' spreading influence in one way or another. Much of the livelihood was dependent on the sea (for the obvious reason that water is surrounding the islands), though we do read of meat being consumed, as we do some other prominent produce distinct to these islands. I will not exhaust each island but give an overview of some regions and their recipes. Combinations of flavors and influences are seen. As noted above the food dependent on the sea belongs to islands such as Kalimnos, Chalki, Simi and Rhodes. Karpathos and Kasos also get their food influence from Asia Minor and Africa, and a little touch from Cyprus and Crete.

Distinctly characteristic on these islands are the blue and white colors, replicating the Greek flag—blue and whitewashed walls, crystal blue seas, white windmills against the blue sky. Mention Mykonos and Santorini, and you will find they are the most tourist-attracted destinations portrayed on postcards and on every Greek website. In contrast to the other Greek islands, these regions are rather barren, with rocky terrain, red and black beaches, dry land, and few luscious green trees. Nevertheless, there are many other things that are also striking, through natural resources like chalk and glass lava, marble from Naxos, gold from Sifnos, and bronze from Serifos, which are prominent for boosting trade and the economy on these islands.

So visit Santorini, and you will be blown away by the all-famous and breathtaking sunsets, spectacular pathways, and white and blue buildings hanging off the cliffs. Then dine in a *taverna* and be welcomed by regional produce that grows exceptionally well. Diversity of produce is brought forth from volcanic soil. Remarkably, this soil maintains incredible minerals and vitamins, which help produce the tastiest capers, fava beans (yellow lentils), white (*Asyrtiko*) wine, and cherry tomatoes. Who would have thought that Santorini is known for these and, more so, its cherry tomatoes? First sown in 1818 by a monk named Fragkiskos at the Capuchins Monastery, tomatoes were in abundance then and have never been altered with any other variety since that time. During the twentieth century, there were 20,000 acres of land that cultivated tomatoes and a tomato paste production center that flourished. Santorini's tomato cultivation thrived until an earthquake occurred in 1956. Thereafter, tourism became more prominent rather than cultivating tomatoes. Though the cultivation is not what it was prior to the earthquake, there remain plenty of delicious cherry tomatoes to consume and a factory in Monolithos that sells these tasty fruits, carefully canned.

A specialty dish that is served on these islands is *kakavia* (*psarosoupa*), meaning "fish soup." Though made throughout other regions, Santorini is most commonly known for it with the addition of saffron, another spice grown on the island. Go to Lesvos, and you find enormous olive groves, sardines, capers, and ouzo. Ikaria is known for pine honey, oregano, and thyme. Chios is recognized for the intricate and delicate resin mastiha. Cardamom plants come from Rhodes, and grapes, grains, tomatoes, and honey from Kos. Where does one end with such abundance of produce? I know we need to start somewhere….

Tomato Fritters from Santorini

Ντοματοκεφτέδες Σαντορίνης

Serves 11 fritters
20 minutes

The tomato fritter originated in Santorini, although these days it can be seen on many taverna menus around the country. Known as the "meatballs for the poor" (*keftedon ton ftohon*), they are best made when tomatoes are in season and are very ripe. The addition of the sun-dried tomatoes provides the fritters with a lovely, rich tang. Some recipes have the addition of olives, feta cheese, and eggs; however, I think that these are flavorsome enough and the only thing needed is a bowl of Greek yogurt and a splash of lemon juice to serve. These fritters can also be deep-fried for that added crunch.

4 ripe medium tomatoes, roughly chopped

¼ cup sundried tomatoes, roughly chopped

1 tablespoon parsley, chopped

1 tablespoon fresh mint, chopped

¼ cup trahana*

½ teaspoon dried oregano

2 tablespoons olive oil

Salt and pepper to taste

¾ cup all-purpose flour

1 teaspoon baking powder

½ cup water

Olive oil for frying

In a bowl, add all the ingredients except the olive oil for frying. Mix together gently until you have a thick batter consistency.

To shallow-fry, heat the oil in a frying pan. Add spoonfuls of the mixture (flatten slightly so it gets evenly cooked), and fry on each side until golden. It should take a few minutes on each side. Remove and place on a paper towel to drain any excess oil. Serve immediately with yogurt and a dash of lemon juice.

Tip: Ensure the oil is hot enough, otherwise the patties will absorb too much oil.

*See description of Trahana in glossary. Trahana in this case is used to draw any moisture out from the tomatoes and create a crunchy bite to the fritters. Trahana can be substituted with coarse bread crumbs.

Fish Soup with Saffron and White Wine

Κυκλαδική κακαβιά με σαφράν και λευκό κρασί

Serves 8
1.5 hours

Kakavia is a fish soup, more commonly known by the name *psarosoupa*, *psari* meaning "fish," *soupa* meaning "soup." *Kakavi* was the cooking vessel (hence the name kakavia) used in ancient times to cook this hearty soup. Fish stew is made in many ways throughout Greece, some with tomatoes, others with an egg and lemon emulsion, and others with the addition of the spice saffron. Santorini is known for its cultivation of saffron. Saffron plants have three threads per flower, and it is the most expensive spice in the world. Crocus, as it is called in Greece, is derived from the word *croci*, meaning "a thread." Only a few strands are needed to add a delicate flavor and color to the fish stew. Islands surrounded by clear, blue, salty Mediterranean water filled with fresh fish and a land bountiful of saffron flowers combined make the best soup possible! Enjoy!

Aegean Islands

- 1 kg (2.2 lb. or 35.27 oz.) snapper, cleaned and gutted, heads optional*
- 2–3 L (67.6–101 fl. oz.) water
- 2 tablespoons salt
- ½ cup olive oil
- 2 medium onions, finely chopped
- 2 medium carrots, chopped into small cubes
- ¾ cup celery, chopped
- 1 tablespoon fresh parsley, chopped
- 2 bay leaves
- 2 large tomatoes, chopped into bite-size pieces
- 3 medium potatoes, cut into small pieces
- 1 tablespoon thyme leaves, chopped
- 1 cup white wine
- 3–4 threads of saffron
- 1 teaspoon cracked black pepper
- 1 slice of orange rind
- 1 slice of lemon rind

In a large stock pot, place the fish, water, and salt. Bring to a boil, then lower heat, leave partially covered, and simmer for 35–40 minutes.

Remove the fish with a slotted spoon, and then pour the stock into a clean bowl through a sieve. Shred the fish into small portions and set aside.

In a clean pot, sauté the onions in the olive oil. When soft and translucent, add carrots, celery, parsley, bay leaves, tomatoes, potatoes, and thyme. Cook for 5 minutes or until soft. Add the wine and saffron and cook for a further 2 minutes. Pour in the fish stock. Add the pepper and the rind. Allow the soup to cook on low heat, partially covered, for 35 minutes or until potatoes are soft.

Remove the rind. Place the shredded fish back into the soup and serve with a drizzle of lemon juice and a little more olive oil.

*I prefer to make the fish stock with the heads, as they release more flavor.

Split-Pea Puree with Caramelized Onions

Φάβα Σαντορίνης

Serves 4-6
1 hour approximately
Gluten-Free

Yellow split peas are what Greeks call *fava*, originating from the Latin word *favus*, meaning "broad bean." This dish was first made with broad beans, which later were replaced with yellow split peas, otherwise known as yellow lentils. As common as pasta is in Italy, fava is in Santorini. The fava beans grow in abundance and have an exceptional taste due to the volcanic soil and are very high in protein. This is much like a dip or spread. There is a similar dish called bissara, which originated in Egypt and is readily available in Morocco but has the consistency between a dip and a soup and is made with cilantro and parsley or cumin as the main spice. The Greek version is eaten fresh in summer, with caramelized onions and capers (another common ingredient on this island), and in winter, it is served with smoked pork, namely *kabourma*. It can be eaten as an entrée and is a great accompaniment to fish or meat. When it cools, it thickens but can be loosened by mixing through a little more olive oil.

¾ cup olive oil, divided

½ medium white onion, finely chopped

1 small carrot, cut into small pieces

1 bay leaf

Salt to taste

½ teaspoon castor (superfine) sugar

1½ cups yellow split peas, rinsed and drained

1 L (33.81 fl. oz.) water

1–2 lemons (to taste), juiced

Capers to garnish

½ teaspoon paprika powder

Caramelized Onions:
1 onion, sliced thinly

3 tablespoons olive oil

Salt to taste

1 teaspoon sugar

1 tablespoon balsamic vinegar

Pour half the olive oil in a pot and sauté the white onion, carrot, bay leaf, salt, pepper, and sugar. Once the onion is soft, add the split peas and water. Cover and bring to a boil. Lower heat and simmer, with lid partially off, until the split peas are mushy and the liquid has evaporated by half. Top with water if it is drying out; this should take around 45 minutes on low heat.

Once the peas are totally broken down, remove the bay and blend (in a food processor or using a stick emulsion blender) until smooth. Add lemon juice, extra salt if needed, and remaining olive oil. Blend again to incorporate. Taste and adjust seasoning. Depending on taste, you may want to add more lemon juice. If it is too thick, add a little more olive oil to loosen the mixture.

To caramelize onions: To a frying pan, add 3 tablespoons olive oil. Heat and add the sliced onion. Add some salt and cook on medium heat until soft and caramelized. Do not rush this, so that you have a slowly cooked onion rather than a burnt, raw-tasting ending. Add sugar and balsamic vinegar and cook for a further 1 minute until gooey and glossy. Remove and cool.

Serve split-pea puree at room temperature with a drizzle of olive oil, capers, paprika, and caramelized onions.

Honey Cheesecake from Sifnos

Μελόπιτα Σίφνου

Serves 8-10
1 hour 15 minutes
Gluten-Free

Melopita is an enjoyable honey cheesecake without any crust. It resembles the texture of a Spanish flan, with a lingering honey taste and a subtle lemon kick from the zest. It is simple to prepare and pleasantly light to eat as an after-dinner meal. The most important thing to remember when making this dessert is to have the freshest eggs possible (preferably organic), fresh ricotta cheese, and a good-quality Greek thyme honey. Serve warm with an additional drizzle of honey.

600 g (1.32 lb. or 21.16 oz.) fresh ricotta cheese

4 whole eggs, lightly beaten

1 cup thyme honey

¼ cup castor (superfine) sugar

1 lemon, zested

Icing (confectioners) sugar to serve

Extra honey to serve

Yogurt to serve (optional)

Preheat oven to 180°C (356°F).

Line the bottom of a cheesecake tin (20 cm or 8 in.) with baking paper. Set aside.

In a large bowl (or a stand mixer), add the ricotta cheese, eggs, honey, sugar, and lemon zest. Whisk until smooth and lumps are removed. It will be runny, but it will be fine once it's cooked.

Pour into baking tin and bake for 45–50 minutes or until golden in color (be careful, as the top can burn quickly). Remove from oven and allow to cool for about 30 minutes. Serve warm with a sprinkling of icing sugar and a drizzle of runny honey or yogurt.

Baked Chickpeas with Rosemary

Ρεβύθια φούρνου με δεντρολίβανο (της Καλύμνου)

Serves 6-8
1.5 hours
Gluten-Free

Chickpeas are such a great alternative when wanting to eat a hearty vegetarian meal. They are meaty and take on flavors well. The rosemary and cumin give this dish a beautiful aroma. This dish once again highlights the effortlessness of Greek dishes, with only a few ingredients, all cooked in one pot, creating a great family meal quickly. You can speed up the process by having soaked and cooked the chickpeas the day before, then assemble and bake when desired.

2 cups dried chickpeas*

1 cup olive oil, divided

3 medium red onions, sliced thinly

Salt and pepper to taste

3 tablespoons dried rosemary, chopped

1 teaspoon cumin powder

2 cups tomato puree

2 cups water

8–10 cherry tomatoes, whole

Couscous or rice to serve

Crumbled feta cheese to serve

*Canned chickpeas can be substituted for dried. Just omit the soaking and preboiling steps.

Soak chickpeas in water overnight or for a minimum of 8 hours. Discard the water and place into a pot covered with fresh water. Bring to a boil and simmer on low heat for 30–35 minutes or until slightly softened but not fully cooked through. Set aside.

Sauté the onions in ½ cup olive oil, with 1 teaspoon salt, until soft and caramelized slightly but not burnt. Add the rosemary and cook for a further 2 minutes. Remove from heat.

Preheat oven to 180°C (356°F). Drain chickpeas.

In a baking dish, spread half the onion mixture on the bottom, then layer chickpeas over the top. Add a sprinkling of salt, pepper, and the cumin powder. Pour over the tomato puree and water. Top with the remaining onions and cherry tomatoes and drizzle over the olive oil. Bake for 1 hour until slightly golden, juices have evaporated, and the olive oil has surfaced to the top. It will be relatively dry.

Serve on a large platter, layering a bed of couscous or rice on the bottom, then a layer of chickpeas sprinkled with feta cheese and a drizzle of olive oil. Juice of one lemon can be added over the whole plattered dish for that extra zing. Can be eaten warm or cold.

Aegean Islands

Chicken and Chickpea Stew

Serves 4-6
1.5 hours
plus 10 hours overnight soaking
Gluten-Free

Κοτόπουλο με ρεβίθια

As seen in the previous recipes, chickpeas are used in various dishes. This is another tasty yet simple dish to make. The only added time is the soaking and cooking of the chickpeas, but you can substitute dried chickpeas with canned if you are short on time. This is a nutritious meal made in one pot and fragrantly seasoned with wine, paprika, and chili. Feel free to increase the amount if you like food hot and spicy. This is very mild.

- 2 cups chickpeas, soaked overnight*
- ¾ cup olive oil, divided
- 1 kg (2.2 lb. or 35.27 oz.) chicken pieces
- 1 large onion, diced
- 1 small leek, chopped
- 1 large carrot, diced
- 1 red capsicum, chopped
- Salt to taste
- 450 g (0.99 lb. or 15.8 oz.) tomato puree
- 1 cup white wine
- 1 teaspoon castor (superfine) sugar
- 2 teaspoon mild paprika powder
- 1 teaspoon chili flakes
- ¼ cup flat-leaf parsley, chopped, to garnish

Drain the soaked chickpeas and add to a saucepan. Pour over enough water to cover. Bring to a boil, then simmer for 30 minutes or until soft. Do not cover the pot, as the chickpeas release a froth when cooking; just skim this off. Drain and set aside in a bowl.

Meanwhile, heat half the olive oil in a wide sauté pan. Add chicken and brown well on all sides. This should take approximately 8–10 minutes. Remove the chicken and set aside. Pour the remaining oil into the saucepan. Add the onion, leek, carrot, capsicum, and salt and sauté on medium heat until the veggies are soft. Place the chicken back into the pan. Add the tomato, wine, sugar, paprika, chili flakes, and cooked chickpeas. Mix well to incorporate. Pour over 1½ cups water, cover with a lid, and simmer for 30–40 minutes.

Chicken should be fully cooked, juices evaporated by half, and olive oil surfaced to the top. Serve warm, scattered with the chopped parsley.

*Canned chickpeas can be substituted for fresh. Omit the initial cooking of the chickpeas. Just add directly into the second stage with the chicken.

Cinnamon Cordial

Κανελάδα (Κῶς)

Serves 6
30 minutes

Kanelada is a beverage drunk all around the island of Kos. It is a cinnamon cordial that is added to ice and water when served, so don't be too worried about the amount of sugar. It is extremely refreshing and served throughout the hot summer months. In some places, red food coloring is added to give the drink a vibrant red color.

2½ cups castor (superfine) sugar

2 cups water

7 cinnamon quills

9 whole cloves

½ a lemon, juiced

1 leaf of lemon geranium, albarosa (optional)

Natural red food coloring (optional)

Place all the ingredients into a pot, stir, and bring to a boil. Reduce heat and simmer for about 20 minutes or until a thick sugar syrup consistency has been achieved. If any foam gathers on top, discard with a ladle. Allow to cool before placing it all into a bottle.

To serve, place ice in a tall glass, strain cinnamon cordial, and pour ¼ cup over the ice. Top with cold water. Taste and adjust (adding more cordial) if you prefer it sweeter.

This syrup is also lovely over vanilla ice cream.

Yogurt-Coated Pasta with Caramelized Onions and Cheese

Μακαρούνες της Κάσσου

Serves 4
25-30 minutes

This is an authentic recipe from the region of Kasou. Homemade pasta was made by the woman of the household, then cooked and coated in *sitaka* (a Kasion cheese), then served with caramelized onions. Obviously, this cheese is hard to find outside of Greece, so Greek yogurt is substituted, giving this dish the slight sourness needed to balance the whole dish. I have also used ready-made dry pasta. This is simple yet comforting at best! Best eaten immediately!

½ cup olive oil

2 large white onions, finely sliced

Salt to taste

250 g (0.55 lb. or 8.81 oz.) short pasta of choice

1 cup yogurt

1 cup grated Kefalotyri cheese*, plus a little more to serve

Pepper to serve

Place olive oil in a wide saucepan and heat. To this, add the onions and salt and sauté until soft and translucent. Do not burn or allow to color. Set aside.

In another pot of boiling salted water, cook pasta until al dente (or as instructed on the packet). Drain pasta into a bowl, reserving the cooking water. Do not overcook pasta.

Take a large bowl and add the yogurt and ½ cup pasta water to loosen the yogurt. Add the caramelized onion (reserving one-quarter of it for garnish). Add the pasta and cheese and mix well to incorporate. Serve immediately with some cracked pepper, sautéed onion, and extra cheese.

*Kefalotyri cheese is available at Mediterranean grocers. It can be substituted with Parmesan cheese.

Shredded Lamb with Currants and Pine Nuts

Μουούρι Καλύμνου

Serves 6-8
4.5 hours
Gluten-Free

The people in Kalimno make a classic roast using a whole lamb stuffed with liver, rice, and pine nuts and heavily spiced with cinnamon. Symbolically resembling the death and resurrection of Jesus Christ, the lamb is cooked in a sealed clay dish (*mououri*—the vessel used to cook the lamb in ancient times) or an outdoor clay oven (resembling the tomb of Jesus Christ), then opened and eaten on Resurrection Sunday, relating to the resurrection of the Lamb of God, Jesus Christ. One whole lamb is generally used (and cooked for ten hours), but to make this a home-friendly recipe, I have used a leg of lamb that has been boned and is ready to stuff. This is a great Sunday meal, and no, you won't need to wait ten hours.

Filling:
- ¼ cup olive oil
- 1 onion, diced
- 1 tablespoon cinnamon powder
- 1 teaspoon clove powder
- Salt and pepper to taste
- 1 tablespoon tomato paste
- ½ cup red wine
- ½ cup long-grain rice
- 1 cup boiled water
- 100 g (0.22 lb. or 3.52 oz.) fried bacon, chopped*
- ¼ cup parsley, chopped
- ½ cup pine nuts, roasted
- ¼ cup currants
- ¼ cup kefalotyri cheese, cubed

Preheat oven to 150°C (302°F).

To make the filling. Heat the oil in a sauté pan. Add the onion and sauté until soft and caramelized. Add spices and season. Add the tomato paste and wine. Cook on medium heat for 5 minutes, stirring to loosen the paste. Add the rice and water. Cook covered on the lowest heat for 8 minutes (the rice will be three-quarters cooked). Remove from heat. Allow to cool slightly. Add fried bacon.

Stir through the parsley, pine nuts, currants, and cheese. Stuff the lamb and seal it with kitchen string. Place in a baking dish. Season and rub lamb with the tomato paste. Pour over lemon juice, olive oil, oregano, and rosemary. Cover well with aluminum foil. Bake for 3–4 hours. Uncover and bake for another 15 minutes so that the lamb goes golden. Shred the meat and serve with the stuffing, potato mash, and a side salad.

*I have substituted livers (from the traditional recipe) with bacon.

1 leg (or shoulder) of lamb, bone removed (1 kg or 2.2 lb.)

Salt and pepper to taste

1 tablespoon tomato paste

2 lemons, juiced

¼ cup olive oil

1 tablespoon dried oregano

1 tablespoon rosemary, chopped

Grilled Octopus

Serves 4
3 hours
Gluten-Free

Χταπόδι στην σκάρα

What is a Greek cookbook without grilling fish? This recipe can also be made using baby octopus. It is best left to marinate overnight, then grilled on hot coals or a hot pan.

Rinse the octopus and place in a large saucepan together with the wine. Half-cover with the lid and allow to come to a boil, then simmer on low heat for 2 hours. Drain and rinse. Cover and refrigerate for a minimum 30 minutes. Cut the legs away from the head, leaving the legs whole.

Prepare the grill.

In a bowl, whisk together the olive oil, oregano, lemon, salt, and pepper. Add the octopus and allow to marinate for a minimum of 20 minutes. Place octopus onto the hot grill, brushing with additional marinade. Cook for a few minutes on each side. Place on a serving plate and serve immediately with some extra lemon juice and a Greek salad.

1 large octopus, whole, cleaned, and tenderized (approximately 1 kg or 2.2 lb. or 35.27 oz.)

2 cups red or white wine

1½ cups olive oil

3 tablespoons Greek oregano, dried

3 lemons, juiced

Salt and pepper to taste

Pan Fried Red Mullet

Μπαρμπούνια τηγανιτά

Serves 3
30-40 minutes

This is a quintessential recipe for frying fish simply and quickly. Fried red mullet, or *barbounia*, as they are called in Greek, are delicious and easy to prepare. This fish is found in abundance in the Aegean Sea. A quick fry ensures the fish does not absorb too much oil and therefore eliminates it from becoming too soggy. Serve immediately, with a glass of chilled ouzo, ensuring you eat the crispy head and tail.

2 cups all-purpose flour

9 red mullet, cleaned, gutted, scaled, heads intact

Salt and pepper to taste

Olive oil for frying

3 lemon wedges to serve

Heat oil in frying pan.

Place flour into a large bowl and season well with salt and pepper. Coat fish with the flour and dust off any excess. Place into the hot oil and fry on medium heat, turning once, until golden on both sides. Place on paper towel to drain any oil. Serve with a side of lemon wedges and a salad.

New Year's Cake

Βασιλόπιτα τσουρέκι

Serves 16 pieces
3.5 hours

Vasilopita is the traditional New Year's Cake! This recipe is a combination between a brioche, a *tsoureki*, and a Christmas bread. It is best eaten the day it is made, though it keeps well for a few days in the refrigerator. Basil of Caesarea, otherwise known as Saint Basil the Great, according to Christian history, is the reason this traditional cake was developed. Custom states that whoever gets the coin once the cake is cut will have good luck throughout the year. The truth is, I am not superstitious, nor do I believe luck is achieved through this means. The Holy Bible states that luck is not what we rely on or need; rather, just as Basil the Great himself states, we need to know the Living God. *"We must possess the hope of eternal glory, which is the gift of God, given only to those who humble themselves and accept it. It cannot be achieved through human effort."* Basil goes on to say, *"Escape from the condemnation due our sins, if we believe in the grace of God given through his only begotten Son."*

75 g (0.16 lb. or 2.64 oz.) currants, dried

40 mL (1.35 fl. oz.) whiskey* or mastiha liquor

75 g (0.16 lb. or 2.64 oz.) mixed peel**

2 oranges, zested

1 lemon, zested

2 teaspoons ground mahlepi†

½ teaspoon ground mastic resin†

½ teaspoon ground cardamom seeds

200 mL (6.76 fl.oz.) whole milk, lukewarm

1 tablespoon yeast

200 g (0.44 lb. or 7.05 oz.) castor (superfine) sugar

6 whole eggs, beaten

½ teaspoon baking powder

4½ cups all-purpose flour

120 g (0.44 lb. or 4.23 oz.) butter at room temperature, chopped into small pieces

A coin that has been wrapped in aluminum foil

Line the base and the sides of a cheesecake tin (20 cm or 7.8 in.) with parchment paper, exceeding the height of the tin by 10 cm (3.93 in.). In a bowl, place the currants, liquor of choice, mixed peel, and zests. Set aside to soak while preparing the rest of the cake.

Attach the paddle attachment to a stand mixer. In the mixer bowl, add mahlepi, mastic resin, cardamom, milk, yeast, and sugar. Mix to just combine. Then add eggs, baking powder, and flour, beating on medium speed for 15 minutes. The batter will be quite runny, so do not be alarmed. Add the butter and the liquor-soaked mix. Mix for another 10 minutes or until the butter is well incorporated. Pour batter into the prepared baking tin. Place the coin somewhere inside the mixture. The mixture will be slightly runny and gooey.

Cover with a clean towel and allow the cake to rise (until doubled in size, approximately 2 hours). Preheat oven to 160°C (320°F). Bake for 80–90 minutes or until a skewer inserted comes out clean. Allow to cool, then dust with icing sugar. It can be stored in an airtight container in the fridge for 3 days.

*Whiskey can be substituted with an orange liquor.
**Mixed peel is a combination of candied orange and lemon piths. It can be purchased from all grocers.
†Mahlepi and mastic resin can be purchased from Mediterranean grocers.

Tip: Chocolate chips can be added right at the end of mixing, for those who love chocolate.

Baked Sardines

Σαρδέλες στο φούρνο

Serves 4-6
55 minutes
Gluten-Free

Sardines are so plentiful in Greece. Commonly eaten with the head and tail intact, this fish is wonderful both fried and baked. Most people avoid sardines because of their strong smell, but this should not be the case when the fish is fresh and cooked well. Throughout Greece, sardines are a common appetizer, or a meze, as it's known, served with a splash of lemon juice and a glass of ouzo liquor.

¾ cup olive oil, divided

1 red capsicum, sliced lengthwise

1 medium red onion, sliced

Salt and pepper to taste

15 large sardines, cleaned and gutted

1 tablespoon dried oregano

3 garlic cloves, minced

½ cup parsley, chopped

2 lemons, zested and juiced

1 cup water

Pour half the olive oil into a baking dish. Place the red capsicum on the bottom of the dish, then layer the onion on top of that. Season with some salt. Layer the sardines over the top of the onion. Scatter the oregano, garlic, parsley, and lemon zest. Pour over the lemon juice, remaining oil, and water. Season with salt and pepper.

Bake uncovered at 180°C (356°F) for 30–35 minutes or until fish is cooked and veggies have softened. Serve warm with a glass of ouzo.

Thessalia
Έβδομο 07

The Valley

One cannot omit the most prevalent and obvious natural phenomenon that exists in Thessalia, far beyond even entering the city—that is, the Meteora. They are rock formations at the heart of the beautiful landscape of central Greece. Twenty-four monasteries (of which six remain active, housing ten people in total) are seen afar, suspended in the air. The monasteries were built for Orthodox monastic communities of the fourteenth century to hide for safety in the face of Turkish attacks in Greece. Today they boast thousands of visiting tourists and locals for their absolute serenity and beauty. Geographically, Thessalía is situated west of Mount Olympus and East of Mount Pelios, where the snowy mountains stand tall.

It has much similarity with the cooking produce of Epiros, though it also has seafood. Organically, it has the best of all, from the mountains, the sea, the rivers, and the plains. Nowhere else in Greece is there such a liking for beef, due to a terrain perfect for cattle ranching. The west has corn as a staple crop and makes use of butter and lard as the fat used in cooking, whereas the east is plentiful in olive groves, making olive oil the preferred ingredient to use in cooking. A few specialties in this region due to the production of corn are *halva farsalon*, a dessert made with cornstarch and topped with a burnt-sugar crust, and the savory corn-crusted spinach pie called *plastos*. Wheat is also a common ingredient grown in this region, and with this, they make *trahana* incomparable to other regions of Greece. The exceptional milk and wheat produce some of the country's tastiest varieties. Trahana is a pebble-shaped pasta made with semolina, bulgur, or cracked-wheat flour mixed together with milk or yogurt and broken up into small pieces, then left outside to dry in the hot sun. Used in many meals, pies and soups, it is a very hearty and healthy ingredient.

Cheese is also very prominent in Thessalía. Beautiful yellow cheeses are served and exported, as are the known meat sausages spiced with paprika and cumin.

Caramel Jelly Pudding with Almonds

Χαλβάς Φαρσάλων

Serves 12 pieces
15 minutes
Gluten-Free

There are three variations of halva in Greece. One is made with semolina flour, the second with sesame paste, and the other with cornstarch. This recipe comes from the town Farsala in the region of Thessalía. It is the cornstarch dessert, with a jelly consistency and sweetened with a semisweet caramel. The origins suggest that this dessert came from the Turks who had settled in Greece in the mid-1400s. The original recipe is made with butter, but I have substituted it with olive oil to keep the saturated fats as low as possible and to highlight the versatility and taste of olive oil.

¼ cup light olive oil

1 cup corn flour (cornstarch)

¼ teaspoon cinnamon powder

2 cups water

1½ cups castor (superfine) sugar, divided, plus 2 tablespoons

¾ cup roasted whole almonds (skins removed)

In a bowl, add olive oil, corn flour, cinnamon powder, and water. Whisk to combine and set aside.

Place a heavy-based stainless-steel pot on the stove on low-to-medium heat. Add half the sugar and allow to heat without stirring. As it starts to brown and caramelize, add the remaining sugar. Allow to melt and brown slightly. You want a deep brown caramel. Do not burn the caramel—keep a close eye on it, otherwise the final dish will taste burnt. Immediately pour in corn flour mixture, mixing vigorously with a wooden spoon. Stand back, as it will splatter. Keep stirring on medium heat until the mixture becomes one gelatinous mass and it comes away from the sides of the saucepan. Pour in almonds and mix through. Set aside.

Lightly oil a nonstick baking tray (24 cm x 12 cm or 9.4 in. x 4.7 in.). Pour in mixture and level it nicely with a spatula. Sprinkle another 2 tablespoons castor sugar over the top. Place tray under a hot grill (or use a blow torch), and allow the sugar on top to caramelize for 10 minutes. Remove from grill and allow to cool for one hour before slicing.
This is best eaten cold with a cup of Greek coffee. It lasts covered in the fridge for up to two days and tastes great the day after!

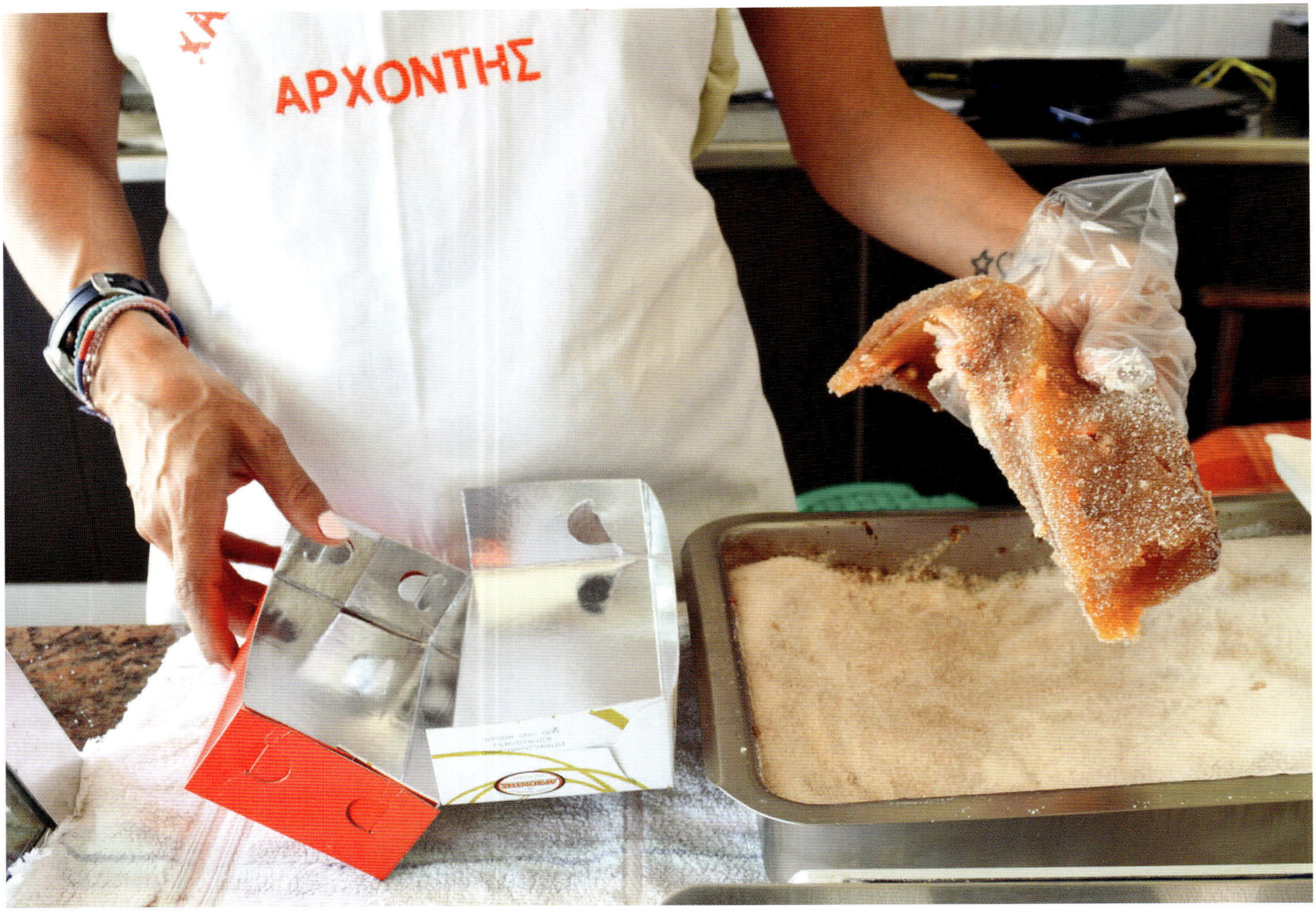
ΑΡΧΟΝΤΗΣ

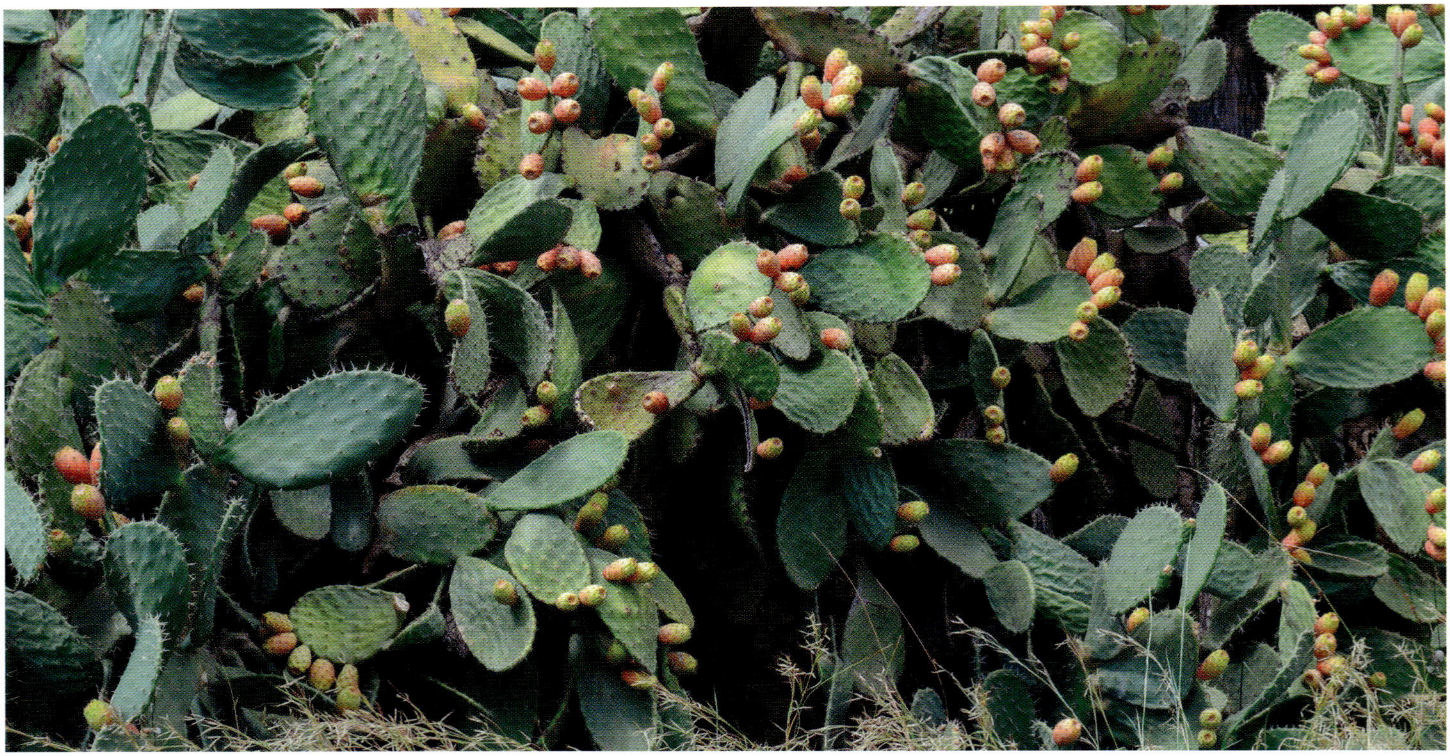

Roast Beef with Vegetables and Melted Cheese

Κελαϊδή μοσχάρι

Serves 5
1 hour 20 minutes
Gluten-Free

Origins of this dish come from Tyrnavos, a city in Larissa. This region is known for the largest carnival festival in central Greece. Usually made from brisket (*spala*), *kelaidi* car also be made using other cuts of meat. All the ingredients are placed in one dish and slowly baked on low heat, without needing much else. Cubes or slices of kefalotyri or kasseri cheese are added at the very end to add that salty, oozy, and cheesy bite. Your house will smell like pizza!

½ cup olive oil, divided

500 g (1.1 lb. or 17.63 oz.) veal or beef cutlets

Salt and pepper to taste

1 large onion, sliced

2 green capsicums, sliced

2 red capsicums, sliced

4 medium tomatoes, sliced in thin, circular shape

5 whole garlic cloves

½ cup water

8–10 thin slices kasseri or kefalograviera cheese*

Preheat oven to 180°C (356°F).

This dish is best made in a clay pot or dutch oven or, alternatively, a well-sealed baking dish.

Drizzle half the olive oil on the bottom of the baking dish. Place the meat to cover the base. Season with salt and pepper. Scatter the onions over the meat, then the capsicums, tomatoes, and garlic. Season again with salt and pepper. Drizzle the remaining oil and add the water. Cover dish with lid or seal well with aluminum foil. Bake on low heat for 1 hour. After an hour, remove from oven and place cheese slices over the top (ensure it is totally covered with cheese).

Bake uncovered until cheese has melted and the juices have almost evaporated from the tray. Remove from oven and serve with mashed potatoes.

*Kasseri or kefalograviera cheese can be purchased from Mediterranean grocers.

Cornmeal Spinach Pie with No Pastry

Πλαστός

Serves 20 pieces
1 hour 20 minutes

This humble dish eventuated during extreme poverty after war times in the years 1930–1940. Flour was becoming scarce, although cornmeal was in abundance. Homemakers would use their imaginations in making bread-like products but with the use of cornmeal, water, a little oil, and salt. The result was something to this effect to feed families in hope of survival. Today it is made without the tensions and fears of hard times and war. This was and is eaten in other areas of Greece with slight differences in the filling and known by different names: *mpatsaria*, *kalabokopsomo*, *bobota*, *tirnabo* and *plastos*. Each name represents what the pie incorporates or, like this one, the use of the plasti or not. What Greeks call plasti is the thin wooden dowel we use to make filo dough. Plastos in this case indicates the omission of not using it at all. This pie has no filo dough but rather a thick batter, which becomes a casing for the spinach filling. Filled with aromatic herbs, fresh spinach, and cheese, this is a very tasty and easy pie to make. The trahana adds a nice crunch to the filling.

Filling:

500 g (0.66 lb. or 10.58 oz.) spinach (or other green leafy vegetables), washed and roughly chopped

¼ cup leeks, finely chopped

2 spring onions, finely chopped

¼ cup mint, chopped

¼ cup parsley, chopped

1 whole egg, lightly beaten

3 tablespoons trahana*

170 g (0.37 lb. or 5.99 oz.) feta cheese, crumbled

150 g (0.33 lb. or 5.29 oz.) kefalotyri or Parmesan cheese, grated

Salt and pepper to taste

2 tablespoons olive oil

Preheat oven to 190°C (374°F).

Place all the filling ingredients into a bowl and mix well to combine. Set aside.

To prepare the bottom crust: In another bowl, add the oil, cornmeal, semolina, and salt and mix with fingers, then add the water and mix until a wet-sand texture is achieved.

Line a baking dish (30 cm x 23 cm or 11.8 in. x 9 in.) with parchment paper. Spread the cornmeal mixture and flatten with a palette knife to cover the base of the pan. Spread the spinach filling over the top, ensuring it is evenly distributed.

For the top crust: In a bowl, mix together the 100 g (0.22 lb. or 3.52 oz.) cornmeal and 125 mL (4.22 fl. oz.) of water. Mix and pour this over the filling. It won't cover the spinach entirely, but it will cover most of it. Then combine the remaining cornmeal and semolina (no water) and spread this over the top. Combine the olive oil and remaining water and drizzle over the top slowly with a spoon to cover the entire area. Sprinkle over some salt and cracked black pepper.

Bake for 45 minutes or until golden and crisp on the top and bottom.

Serve warm or at room temperature.

*See description of trahana in glossary.

Bottom Crust:
100 mL (3.38 fl. oz.) olive oil

200 g (0.44 lb. or 7.05 oz.) cornmeal (polenta)

100 g (0.22 lb. or 3.52 oz.) semolina flour

½ teaspoon salt

150 mL (5.07 fl. oz.) tepid water

Top Crust:
160 g (0.35 lb. or 5.64 oz.) cornmeal (polenta), divided

250 mL (8.45 fl. oz.) tepid water, divided

60 g (0.13 lb. or 2.11 oz.) semolina flour

100 mL (3.38 fl. oz.) olive oil

Salt to taste

Pepper to taste

Cornmeal Spinach Pie with No Pastry, page 197.

Soup with Trahana

Τραχανόσουπα

Serves 6-8
35 minutes

Trahana is an ancient food! It is otherwise known as *xinohondros, xinos* meaning "sour," and *hondros* meaning "dehulled wheat grain." It is made from cracked wheat or bulgar, salt, flour, and yogurt or sour milk, which are left to ferment in the dry, hot summer sun, usually during the month of August. In its dry form, it resembles a small pasta. When liquid is added, it becomes like a thick porridge. Once it is cool or placed in the fridge, it solidifies slightly yet still retains a lovely semi-loose, gelatinous texture. I enjoy the simplicity of this soup. It has few ingredients, enhanced by a good helping of mizithra, feta, or Parmesan cheese. As with various foods, there is usually some story or tale to accompany the origins of how it got its name. Through the Ottoman reign, once again the sultan (priest), having visited a household, was offered to sit and enjoy a meal. What was cooked on that day was this very humble soup, called *dar hane*, which basically means "soup of the household." Since then and throughout the years, its name was transformed to *tarhana*, and in Greek, "trahana."

1/3 cup olive oil

1 small onion, minced

2 cups tomato puree

2 L (67.62 fl. oz.) boiled water

1 teaspoon salt

½ teaspoon ground paprika

1¾ cups trahana (xinos)*

1 bay leaf

Mizithra, Parmesan, or feta cheese to serve

Heat oil in a large pot. Add the onion and sauté for 3 minutes. Add the tomato puree and mix well. Add boiled water, salt, paprika, trahana, and bay leaf. Simmer uncovered on a low heat for 20 minutes (make sure to stir regularly so the trahana does not stick to the bottom of the pot). Cook until the soup has thickened slightly and the trahana is cooked. It should be al dente. Turn off heat and allow to rest, covered, for 10 minutes before serving.

Serve in bowls while hot, sprinkled with grated mizithra or crumbled feta cheese. The soup will thicken into a slightly gelatinous consistency. It can be eaten like that or reheated with an additional ½ cup water to loosen the texture.

*See description of trahana in glossary.

Trahana Pie with No Pastry

Τραχανόπιτα χωρίς φύλλο

Serves 12 pieces
45 minutes

As seen on the previous page, trahana can be used in soups, stews, and pies. This recipe is a no-pastry pie, similar to that of a cheese slice with the added texture of the trahana. I like the noncomplexity of this recipe. Just grab a bowl, mix together the ingredients, bake, and eat! Simple, healthy, and delicious!

1 cup whole milk

1 cup all-purpose flour

1 teaspoon baking powder

3 whole eggs, whisked together

½ teaspoon salt

½ teaspoon black pepper

½ cup sour trahana*

250 g (0.55 lb. or 8.81 oz.) crumbled feta cheese, divided

100 g (0.22 lb. or 3.5 oz.) kefalograviera cheese**

¼ cup olive oil, divided

Preheat oven to 180°C (356°F).

In a bowl, whisk together the milk, flour, and baking powder. Add the beaten eggs, salt, pepper, trahana, 200 g (7.05 oz.) feta, kefalograviera cheese, and half the olive oil. Mix the ingredients well with a wooden spoon. Pour the mixture into an oiled 20 cm (8 in.) round dish. Top with the remaining 50 g (1.7 oz.) feta cheese and drizzle olive oil over the top.

Bake for 35 minutes or until golden. Allow the pie to cool slightly, and then slice and serve it.

*See description of trahana in glossary.

**Kefalograviera cheese can be substituted with Parmesan cheese.

Chicken Livers with Egg and Lemon

Συκωτάκια με αυγό και λεμόνι

Serves 4
1 hour
Gluten-Free

If you are not a fan of chicken livers, you must try this recipe. I can assure you it wll change your mind. The fried egg and lemon juice cut through the liver, leaving a very pleasant flavor. If you didn't know that the livers were the primary ingredient, you would never have guessed it while eating it. They are fragrant and tasty. This dish is best served with rice.

800 g (1.76 lb. or 28.21 oz.) chicken livers, cleaned

¼ cup olive oil

Salt to taste

3 whole eggs, beaten

1 tablespoon dried oregano

2 lemons, juiced

Remove any skin from the chicken livers and wash extremely well. Place in a wide pan covered with fresh water. Bring to a boil, then drain and repeat. Place back into the pot and cover with fresh water, oil, and salt. Boil on medium heat until all the water has evaporated and the oil has surfaced to the top. Now add the lemon juice.

Beat eggs in a bowl and slowly pour over the livers. Gently toss with a spatula to cover all the livers and for the egg to cook through. Add oregano over the top, turn off heat, and serve. Extra lemon juice can be added if desired.

Spicy Stew of Peppers, Sausage, and White Wine

Serves 4
1 hour 20 minutes
Gluten-Free

Σπετσοφάι με χωριάτικο λουκάνικο

The original recipe comes from the city of Volos and Pelion villages. It is usually made with hot peppers and spicy sausages (though it can be made using a nonspicy variety). The name of this dish comes from the word *spetses*, meaning a mixture of peppers. It is simplistic in ingredients yet packs a punch of flavor. Use crisp peppers, a good-quality sausage, and always the best extra-virgin olive oil. As with all Greek meals, a hearty bread loaf (omit for gluten-free), a serving of feta cheese, and a glass of ouzo are the best accompaniment.

¼ cup olive oil

2 spicy (optional) pork sausages, sliced into 1-cm (0.39-in.) pieces

1 medium onion, sliced

2 garlic cloves, sliced

1 red capsicum, sliced into 1-cm (0.39-in.) strips

2 green capsicums, sliced into 1-cm (0.39-in.) strips

1 small chili pepper (optional), sliced into 1-cm (0.39-in.) rounds

2 cups tomato puree

1 cup white wine

½ cup water

Salt and pepper to taste

In a wide pan, heat the oil and add the sausages. Brown on both sides, then remove and set aside. With the juices from the sausages still in the pan, add the onion and garlic. Cook on medium heat until the onion has softened and slightly caramelized. Add back the sausages and all the peppers. Sauté for 3 minutes, then add the tomato puree, wine, and water and season with salt and pepper.

Simmer on low for 20–35 minutes or until the peppers are soft and the juices have thickened. Serve hot or at room temperature.

Spiced Walnut Cake with a Vanilla Custard Topping

Σπάτουλα Καλαμπάκας:
Καρυδόπιτα με κρέμα

Serves 20-30 pieces
3-4 hours including
cooling time

This is a dessert you will most commonly find in the region of Thessalía, with various names such as *spatoula*, *poutinga*, or *kofti*. Spatoula refers to using a large spoon to eat it due to the copious amounts of custard. Some make a slightly runnier custard so that it runs down the cake. I prefer it thicker so that the pieces can be cut easier and the custard sits nicely over the top. The pride and staple in Kalabaka is their remarkable milk, derived from the cattle grazing on the mountains. This cake is a showcase of Kalabaka's milk production through the thick custard sitting pridefully on the top. It is a spiced walnut cake that is drenched in syrup, then topped with vanilla custard. It is refreshing and not overly sweet. Give yourself plenty of time to allow each layer to cool. It is a crowd-pleaser that can be made a day in advance.

Sponge:
¾ cup self-rising flour

1 teaspoon cinnamon powder

1 cup walnuts, coarsely crushed

¼ teaspoon clove powder

1 teaspoon baking powder

½ an orange, zested

5 whole eggs, room temperature

¾ cup castor (superfine) sugar

Syrup:
1½ cups castor (superfine) sugar

1½ cups water

2 tablespoons koniak or liquor of choice

For the sponge: Preheat oven to 170°C (338°F). Place the flour, cinnamon, walnuts, clove powder, baking powder, and zest of orange in a bowl. Set aside. In a mixer, add the eggs and sugar. Beat on high for 15 minutes or until thick and pale. Remove from mixer, and with a wooden spoon incorporate the flour mixture very slowly, ensuring to not overmix.

Pour into a well-buttered baking dish (32 cm x 24 cm or 13.3 in. x 9.4 in.) and bake for 30–40 minutes. It will come away from the sides of the baking pan once it is cooked. Allow to cool.

To make the syrup, place the sugar and water in a pot. Bring to a boil, then simmer for 6 minutes. Remove from heat and add liquor. Slowly pour hot syrup over cold cake using a soup ladle, starting from the outer edges and working toward the middle. Allow it to cool completely.

To make the cream, place the milk in a pot. Heat well but do not boil. In a separate bowl, add the flour, sugar, vanilla and eggs. Whisk together, then add one cup of the heated milk. Whisk, then pour this mixture into the milk. Keep whisking on low heat until a thickened custard has been achieved. It should be at boiling point. Remove from heat and add the vanilla powder. Place a piece of cling film directly onto the cream and allow it to cool completely. Once custard is cool, mix through the whipped cream.

Pour custard-cream over the cooled cake. Allow to set in the fridge for at least a few hours before serving. To serve, sprinkle additional walnuts over the top and sprinkle with cinnamon powder. It can be stored in the refrigerator, covered, for three days.

Custard:

1 L (33.8 fl. oz.) whole milk

100 g (0.22 lb. or 3.52 oz.) all-purpose flour

¾ cup castor (superfine) sugar

2 whole eggs

1 teaspoon vanilla powder

2 cups thickened whipped cream

Spiced Walnut Cake with a Vanilla Custard Topping, page 209.

Sesame Pie

Σουσαμόπιτα

Serves 20 pieces
1 hour plus overnight resting

Sesame has long been an ingredient of the Thessalian diet. Barley, wheat, pulses, and sesame seeds grow abundantly in this region. Thessalía has also been known as the "wheat belt of Greece." This dessert is found only in this region. The ground sesame gives it a great texture, and the spicing is aromatic and intense. It resembles the taste of baklava but without the added fats (being the copious amounts of sugar and butter). If you prefer a sweeter and moister version, just double the syrup ingredients.

2 cups sesame seeds, browned*

1 cup walnuts, crushed

2 tablespoons cinnamon powder

½ tablespoon clove powder

8 sheets filo pastry, store-bought

16 whole cloves

¾ cup olive oil

Syrup:
2½ cups water

2½ cups castor (superfine) sugar

1 tablespoon honey

1 lemon rind

1 orange rind

*To brown sesame, place sesame seeds in a dry skillet on medium heat and stir continuously for 5–10 minutes. It burns very quickly, so keep an eye on it.

Grease a baking tray with a little olive oil, or line with greaseproof paper.

Using a food processor or grinder, pulse the browned sesame 2–3 times to crush slightly. Do not pulse too many times, as you want some sesame to remain semi-whole. In a bowl, place the sesame, walnuts, cinnamon, and clove powder. Mix to combine.

You will need 4 sheets of pastry for each log. Take one sheet of pastry and scatter a few tablespoons of nut filling over the top. Place another sheet of filo directly on top, repeating with the same amount of filling until all four are done. Then roll it up into a sausage, starting from the edge closest to you. Gently lift and place onto baking tray. Repeat this with the remaining filo pastry until you have two rolls on the baking tray. With a serrated knife, gently cut (halfway through) each log (diagonally) into 10 pieces. Place a clove on each piece.

In a pot, bring the olive oil to a boil. Remove from heat and spoon over the pastry, ensuring that it makes a sizzling sound (if not, heat more). Bake for 15–20 minutes. Allow to cool completely.

Place all the syrup ingredients into a pot. Bring to a boil, then lower heat and simmer for 9 minutes, then pour over cooled pastry. Allow the syrup to seep into the pastry approximately 5 hours or preferably overnight. Serve with coffee or some vanilla or cinnamon ice cream.

The heart of Ancient Greece is Athens! The capital city encapsulates history, the birthplace of democracy, a powerful civilization and empire, and a city full of ancient ruins, museums and temples. Visit Athens and you will see not only much richness of history, but you will also experience hospitality, the Greek way of eating and sharing food. Athens restaurants and tavernas are filled with locals eating and drinking very leisurely and in an unhurried manner. Food here is not a very specific type, per se, but rather a good representation of what Greece has to offer as a whole. For breakfast you can eat bread rings (*koulouria*), a bowl of Greek yogurt served with honey and some spoon sweet, or various spinach and cheese pastries, followed by a main taverna meal and finishing off with a Greek coffee or Freddo Cappuccino. There is such a variety in this city! Everything you find in Athens is commonly a fusion of produce gathered from all parts of Greece and heavily influenced by other European cuisines. However, the Attika area does produce some exquisite thyme, thyme honey, wine (made into Metaxas brandy), and pistachios.

Piraeus, the largest port in Greece, is just a half-hour drive from Athens City. It is historically the home of the Athenian Navy. Culinarily, this port is the oasis for fish and seafood to be shipped from all around Greece. The fast food *souvlaki* is served at every corner. Whether one buys the shredded meat or the *kalamaki* (meat on a stick), this tantalizing meal is healthy and delicious. The meat is spiced to perfection, served on pita bread, and smothered in tzatziki, fried potatoes, slices of tomato, lettuce, and onions—all wrapped into a delicate wrap. Athens is a place to get all meze meals, to whet one's appetite for all that Greece has to offer.

fusion foods

Greek Yogurt Panacotta with Honey

Πανακότα με μέλι

Serves 8
4 hours
Gluten-Free

Panacotta is an Italian word for "cooked cream." Panacotta has made its way into many households around the world, including Greece, with some slight adaptations to the original recipe. Here the cream is diluted with Greek yogurt, adding a slight sourness to balance the sweet, and is served with Greek honey and a pistachio praline. Central Greece is known for its pistachio trees and thyme honey. This honey is filled with nutritional properties; contains antibacterial, antiviral and antifungal substances; and is loaded with vitamins, minerals, and antioxidants.

Attiki

400 mL (13.52 fl. oz.) thickened cream (heavy cream)

4 tablespoons castor (superfine) sugar

¼ teaspoon mastiha powder* (or one vanilla bean, seeded)

3 sheets gelatin (60 g or 0.13 lb. or 2.82 oz.)

500 g (1.1 lb. or 17.6 oz.) yogurt

Runny honey to serve

Pistachio Praline:
200 g (0.44 lb. or 7.05 oz.) castor (superfine) sugar

80 g (0.17 lb. or 2.82 oz.) shelled pistachios, crushed

Pinch of salt

Place the cream, sugar, and mastiha powder or vanilla in a pot. Stir to dissolve sugar and bring to a boil, then remove from heat. Soak gelatin in water until soft. Squeeze out any excess water from the gelatin and add to the cream mixture. Mix well, then add the yogurt, whisking until smooth. Strain the mixture through a fine sieve. Divide the mixture into eight ramekins or molds. Chill until set.

To make the caramel for the praline: Line a baking tray with parchment paper. In a small saucepan, add the sugar and melt without stirring. Once a light brown caramel color is achieved, remove from heat and add the pistachios and pinch of salt, mixing quickly to incorporate. Pour this onto the parchment paper and allow it to cool completely. Break into pieces.

To serve, dip the mold into some hot water to help release the panacotta. Run a paring knife around the edges and unmold onto a serving plate. Drizzle with honey, add some pistachio praline, and serve immediately.

*Mastiha powder is available at all European grocers.

Chocolate Log with Orange and Honey

Κορμός με πορτοκάλι και μέλι

Serves 20 pieces
15 minutes to prepare, plus 3-4 hours freezing time

One name of this dessert, *kormos*, is derived from its shape, meaning "tree log," or *mosaico* from the mosaic-looking design it has once it is cut, and another is *salami* if rolled up like a cylinder. So many names and so many variations exist for this dessert. This slice is best made with the famous Greek biscuit called Πτι-Μπερ (*Pti-Ber*), by Papadopoulos biscuits,* a company dated back to the 1930s supplying Greek households in over forty countries worldwide. They are semisweet and retain their shape without becoming too soft. Generally made with cocoa powder, butter, and biscuits, this dessert is one that every household consumes, especially in the summer months. No baking is required, and in literally 15 minutes it can be prepared. It is then placed into the freezer and sliced as desired. It does not freeze but remains cold, so it is ideal to have on hand for the unexpected guests! To add my own extra Greek flavoring, I have added Greek honey and preserves. I have replaced the butter and cocoa with good-quality dark chocolate. This combination is delicious, and the texture is quite moussey.

300 mL (10.14 fl. oz.) thickened cream (heavy cream)

400 g (0.88 lb. or 14.1 oz.) 70% dark chocolate, cut into small pieces

2 large tablespoons runny honey

1½ packets (400 g or 0.88 lb. or 14.1 oz.) Papadopoulos or teddy bear cookies, crushed slightly (keeping 8–10 biscuits whole)*

½ cup hazelnuts, roasted and chopped

¼ cup orange preserve (spoon sweet), chopped, optional**

½ orange, zested

1 cup cocoa powder or icing (confectioners) sugar to dust before serving (optional)

Line a loaf tin (30 cm x 10 cm x 7 cm or 11.8 in. x 3.9 in. x 2.75 in.) with aluminum foil, then a layer of greaseproof paper, allowing an overhang. Set aside.

Heat cream in a pot but do not boil. Add chopped chocolate pieces and mix well until it has completely melted. Add the honey. Mix. In a separate bowl, place crushed biscuit, hazelnuts, preserve, and zest. Pour over melted chocolate. Mix to combine well. Pour mixture into loaf tin and press down to compress. Place whole biscuits on top to create a layer on top. Fold the overhang to cover chocolate log. Refrigerate for a minimum of 4 hours. Remove log onto a chopping board or platter and slice. Keep refrigerated. This dish lasts up to four days.

*Πτι-Μπερ (Pti-Ber) Papadopoulos biscuits are available at Mediterranean delicatessens.

**Orange spoon sweet is available at all Mediterranean delicatessens.

Τζατζίκι

Serves 3 cups
10 minutes
Gluten-Free

Tzatziki recipe taken from my other publication: *Hellenic Kanella: Memories Made in a Greek Kitchen.*

Tzatziki is undeniably our national dip. This refreshing yet garlicky and pungent dip goes well with so many different foods. The flavor develops and intensifies the longer you leave it, so make it a day in advance. It will keep in the fridge for at least four days. Use the best full-cream Greek yogurt you can find. Tzatziki can be used on meat and fish, thickly smeared on some crusty bread, or made as a dip for your favorite chips or crisps. This is my Grandmother Angela's recipe.

3 cups yogurt

½ an English cucumber, peeled, grated, and strained

4 garlic cloves, minced

½ teaspoon salt

1 teaspoon white or red wine vinegar

1 tablespoon olive oil

Place all the ingredients (ensuring the cucumber has been strained well) into a bowl and mix well. Taste and adjust the seasoning.

Serve the tzatziki drizzled with a little olive oil. Refrigerate it, and then use it as desired.

Tip: For an even thicker consistency, you can strain the yogurt in a muslin cloth or tea towel for a few hours prior to assembling the remaining ingredients. Straining reduces the quantity by half.

Souvlaki

Σουβλάκι

Serves 8
1 hour
Gluten-Free*

Every non-Greek wants to know, what's the difference between a gyro and a souvlaki? We need that sorted before we can proceed. *Gyro* is the Greek word for "going around." This is the meat that cooks on a vertical rotisserie. Souvlaki, on the other hand, is meat on a skewer, that is barbecued. Slow-cooked roasted meat can also be used. Think leftover roast lamb or chicken dinner. Shred the meat, heat, and place in the pita as directed below. Traditionally, pork is served in Greece, but feel free to use chicken or lamb.

Place all the ingredients into a bowl. Cover with cling film, refrigerate, and allow to marinate for a minimum of 5 hours or overnight. Soak the skewers in water for a minimum of 30 minutes so that they won't burn during the cooking process. Remove the meat from the fridge. Place onto skewers.

Preheat a barbecue or grill pan. Once hot, coat with a little oil and add the skewers. Cook, turning occasionally until cooked through. Transfer to a plate, add a squeeze of lemon juice and extra salt, and assemble as follows. Place a warmed pita on a serving plate. Add 1–2 tablespoons of tzatziki dip as the base. Add meat, sliced tomatoes, lettuce, and onion. Add optional fries. Wrap and eat!

*Use gluten-free bread for this option.

**If you prefer to use chicken, substitute the vinegar with lemon juice and do not add honey.

Tip: Another lovely combination is adding roasted red bell peppers to the wrap.

1 kg (2.20 lb. or 35.27 oz.) pork shin, cut into bite-size pieces**

2 garlic cloves, minced

¼ cup olive oil

1 teaspoon paprika powder

Salt and pepper to taste

2 tablespoons dried oregano

¼ cup red wine vinegar

2 tablespoons runny honey

1 cup orange juice, freshly squeezed

Skewers or rosemary stalks, soaked in water for a minimum of 30 minutes

To serve:
Pita bread, store-bought

5 tomatoes, sliced

1 head of lettuce, sliced

3 large onions, sliced

Tzatziki dip
(recipe in this chapter)

2 lemon wedges

Potato fries (optional)

Beetroot Salad with Walnut, Apple, Honey, and Yogurt

Παντζαροσαλάτα με καρύδια, μήλα, μέλι και γιαούρτι

Serves 5
35 m nutes
Gluten-Free

Beetroot, yogurt, and walnuts have long been a classic combination in the culinary world of Greece. All three ingredients are used extensively in the kitchen. This salad is fresh with the addition of green apples, slightly sweetened by the Greek honey, and tangy from the yogurt and lemon. It is best eaten cold. Brined beetroot can also be used.

1 kg (2.2 lb. or 35.27 oz.) fresh beetroot, peeled

2½ green apples, peeled and cut into bite-size pieces, divided

Salt to taste

½ cup yogurt

1 lemon, juiced

2½ tablespoons runny honey, divided

¾ cup walnuts, roasted and crushed (not too fine)

1 cup feta cheese, crumbled

1 tablespoon fresh dill, chopped

Place washed and peeled whole beetroot in a pot of salted water. Simmer on medium heat until the beetroot is soft. Remove and allow to cool, then cut into small, bite-size pieces. Place in a serving bowl together with two apples.

In another bowl place yogurt, lemon, and 2 tablespoons of honey, mixing to combine. Add this to the bowl with the beetroot. Gently mix to coat the salad. Place in the refrigerator for a minimum of 30 minutes.

When ready to serve, scatter walnuts, feta cheese, slices of remaining apple (do not mix, so the apple stays bright in color), dill, and more runny honey. It is best eaten cold. Additional lemon juice can be added. Keep refrigerated for up to two days.

Tip: Use gloves when handling beetroot to avoid stains.

Tahini Cake with Chocolate, Honey and Olive Oil

Ταχινόπιτα με σοκολάτα, μέλι και ελαιόλαδο

Serves 6 pieces
45 minutes

Tahini is an unusual ingredient for cakes, but added with chocolate, honey, and olive oil, it becomes a semi-peanut-butter-flavored cake without the peanuts. It's super moist from the olive oil. You can also add chocolate bits into the mix if you want a super gooey cake. Ensure you don't overcook this cake. It should be a cross between a cake and brownie texture.

250 g (0.55 lb. or 8.1 oz.) dark chocolate, cut into small cubes

1 cup olive oil

¼ cup honey

200 g (0.44 lb. or 7.05 oz.) castor (superfine) sugar

4 whole eggs

110 g (0.24 lb. or 3.88 oz.) all-purpose plain flour

1 teaspoon baking powder

30 g (0.06 lb. or 1.05 oz.) cocoa powder

200 g (0.44 lb. or 7.05 oz.) halva, broken into small, bite-size pieces*

80 g (0.17 lb. or 2.82 oz.) tahini paste

*Halva is available at any Mediterranean grocer. Ensure you get the tahini-based halva, not the semolina one, for this recipe.

Preheat oven to 180°C (356°F).

Grease and line a 23 cm (9 in.) square baking tin with baking paper. Set aside. Melt the chocolate in a heatproof bowl over a pan of simmering water, ensuring the base does not touch the water. Once the chocolate has melted, remove the bowl and add to it the olive oil and honey. Whisk to combine and set aside until it has cooled down slightly.

In another bowl, whisk together the sugar and eggs until pale and creamy, roughly 3–5 minutes. Now pour in the melted chocolate mixture and gently fold through, without over-mixing.

Sift the flour, baking powder, and cocoa powder. Gently fold through the chocolate mixture. Now add the halva pieces and pour into the lined baking tin. Pour the tahini paste over the top using a teaspoon, then take a skewer and swirl it through to create a pattern effect over the top.

Bake for 30 minutes or until the sides have cooked and there is a slight wobble in the center. It may seem a little undercooked, but it will firm up once it cools down. If uncertain, cook it a little longer or until a toothpick inserted is mostly dry. Set aside to cool, then cut and serve with vanilla ice cream, crumbled halva pieces, and a drizzle of honey!

Marinated Octopus

Χταπόδι τουρσί

Serves 4-6
1 hour
Gluten-Free

Octopus is traditionally served as a meze with other small plates of food. It is an appetizer eaten with a shot of chilled ouzo liquor. Though I could have easily placed this recipe in any of the Greek island chapters, I added it to central Greece, as it is a very common meze in tavernas all around Athens, as well. The catch of the day comes from Aegina, a small island approximately a 1- to 2-hour ferry ride from Athens. Octopuses are caught, smacked against rocks (to tenderize), then hung to dry in the sun like clothes washing on a line. From there, small boats transport the seafood to mainland tavernas and markets. Source a fresh octopus, and as with most Greek meals, simplicity of ingredients is key!

1 whole octopus (1 kg or 2.2 lb. or 35.27 oz.), cleaned, beak and head removed

2 tablespoons fennel seeds, divided

1¼ cup olive oil, divided

2 tablespoons honey

1 cup red wine vinegar

2 tablespoons capers (optional)

2 garlic cloves, crushed

1 small red chili pepper, sliced (optional)

1 orange, zested

1 lemon, zested

1 teaspoon salt

1 bay leaf

Preheat oven to 200°C (392°F).

Place the whole octopus, 1 tablespoon fennel seed, and ¼ cup olive oil in a baking dish, covered with a lid (or sealed well with two layers of aluminum paper). Do not add any water if you are baking it. The octopus will release its own juices. Bake for 40 minutes.

Alternatively, place ingredients in a covered saucepan (with ½ cup water) and cook on the stove on low heat for 30 minutes or until the octopus is fork-tender. Do not overcook the octopus, otherwise it will be tough. Remove from the saucepan or baking dish and set aside to cool.

Using kitchen scissors or a knife, chop octopus into bite-size pieces and place into a glass jar. Place the honey and vinegar in a bowl and whisk to dilute the honey. Pour this into the jar with the octopus. Add 1 tablespoon fennel seed, capers, garlic, chili, orange and lemon zest, salt, bay leaf, and remaining olive oil. Ensure the octopus is covered, otherwise add more oil. Close jar and shake to incorporate.

Refrigerate for a couple of hours before serving. Keep in the refrigerator. It will last up to one month. Serve with a glass of ouzo.

Baked Patties with Lemon Potatoes

Μπιφτέκια στο φούρνο

Serves 5
1.5 hours
Gluter-Free

Baked meatballs with potatoes are a classic Sunday dish for the whole family. What makes this dish exceptionally tasty is the amount of lemon juice combined with the Greek dried oregano. Do not substitute with any other sort of oregano. You can buy Greek oregano in any Mediterranean grocer or even online. This is a simple but tasty meal that is enjoyed by the old and the young. You can prepare ahead by making the patties a day ahead (then keep covered in the refrigerator). Place peeled and cut potatoes in a bowl of fresh water (inhibits discoloration) until ready to bake.

5–6 medium potatoes, peeled and quartered

½ cup lemon juice

¾ cup olive oil

1½ tablespoons dried oregano

Salt and pepper to taste

2 cups water

Patties:
2 slices of bread, crusts removed

½ cup red wine

1 medium onion, chopped

½ cup olive oil

¼ cup fresh parsley, chopped

1 garlic clove, minced

1 teaspoon cumin powder (optional)

1 whole egg

500 g (1.1 lb. or 17.6 oz.) beef mince (or combination of beef and pork)

Salt and pepper to taste

Sauce to Serve:
2 lemons, juiced

¼ cup olive oil

2 tablespoons parsley, chopped

Preheat oven to 190°C (374°F). Place the potatoes, lemon juice, olive oil, oregano, salt, pepper, and water onto a baking tray. Mix to coat well. Set aside.

Take the bread and tear into small pieces, then place in a bowl with the red wine and allow to soak for 10 minutes. Squeeze out the wine and place the soaked bread into a large bowl. To this add the onion, olive oil, parsley, garlic, cumin, egg, and meat. Season with salt and pepper and mix using your hands to combine everything well.

Divide the mixture into 100 g (0.22 lb. or 3.52 oz.) portions. Making them the same size ensures all the patties cook at the same time. Place the patties on top of the potatoes. Drizzle a little more olive oil over the patties and bake for approximately 50 minutes (turning the patties after about 25 minutes). Cook until potatoes are golden and patties cooked. If the patties cook quicker than the potatoes, remove them from the oven. Cover to keep warm and continue to cook the potatoes until they are crispy and golden.

To serve, whisk together the additional lemon juice, oil, and parsley. Drizzle over patties. Serve with potatoes and a salad.

Spiced Tahini Baklava

Μπακλαβά με ταχίνι

Serves 22 pieces
1 hour plus overnight resting

Sesame is such an intricate ingredient produced in Greece, and the use of it in recipes is unending. Here the sesame is used in its liquid form, tahini (a rich paste made from ground sesame seeds). The end result is slightly fudgy, with a taste similar to peanut butter but without the peanuts. This is a variance again to the traditional baklava and is a delicious crowd pleaser.

Syrup:
1½ cups castor (superfine) sugar
1½ cups water
1 tablespoon honey
1 cinnamon quill

Filling:
1/3 cup castor (superfine) sugar
1½ cups walnuts, crushed
1 orange, zested
1½ teaspoons cinnamon powder
¼ teaspoon clove powder

12 sheets filo pastry, store-bought
1¼ cups tahini paste
2 tablespoons runny honey

Preheat oven to 170°C (338°F).
Prepare the syrup. Place all the ingredients into a pot and bring to a boil. Reduce heat and simmer on low for 10 minutes. Remove from heat and set aside to cool completely.

In a bowl, place the sugar, walnuts, zest, cinnamon, and clove powder. Mix and set aside.

Take a sheet of filo pastry and carefully brush sporadically with (or drop dollops of) tahini paste (it may be a little hard to spread, so you can heat it gently for a few minutes to soften). Top with another sheet of filo and repeat the process until you have 4 sheets nicely on top of each other. Scatter a few tablespoons of nut mixture over the top. Roll up and place seam-side down onto a baking tray. Repeat with another 3 rolls, placing them tightly next to each other on the tray.

In a small bowl, mix any remaining tahini with 1 tablespoon water and honey (you can omit this step if you don't like the tahini browning over the top). Brush over the top of the rolls, then, using a serrated knife, score (half-cut) 22 pieces. Bake for 30–40 minutes or until golden. Remove from oven and immediately pour over the cold syrup. Allow the cake to soak up the syrup (minimum 4 hours or preferably overnight), then cut all the way down and lay the pieces flat-side down so that the syrup penetrates through. After another hour, turn them over so that the other side can also soak up some syrup. Serve with coffee.

Octopus Stew with Pasta

Κοφτό μακαρονάκι με χταπόδι

Serves 4-6
1 hour

Octopus dishes are plentiful in Greece. From winter-warming baked octopus, which is heavily spiced, to the classic, much-loved pickled with a splash of fresh lemon juice, or just plainly cooked on hot coals in the summer. Octopus is usually served as a meze on all the islands, but it's a great main meal served with crusty bread and a glass of wine. The recipe below is a combination of octopus being stewed and baked. Huddled in a spiced ouzo sauce, the octopus becomes tender and extremely aromatic. The slight hint of allspice and the aniseed flavor from the ouzo really accentuate the taste, leaving a beautiful sweet and peppery flavor to the overall dish. Ensure the pasta is not overcooked, otherwise it will become gluggy.

- 1 large octopus (approx. 1 kg or 2.2 lb. or 35.27 oz.), cleaned
- 2 bay leaves
- ¾ cup olive oil, divided
- 1 medium onion, diced
- ½ cup ouzo liquor *
- 1 tablespoon tomato paste
- 1 cup tomato puree
- 6 peppercorns
- 4 allspice berries (pimento, optional)
- Salt to taste
- 2 teaspoons castor (superfine) sugar
- 1 cinnamon quill
- Lemon rind (5-cm or 1.96 in. piece)
- Orange rind (5-cm or 1.96 in. piece)
- 3 cups boiled water
- 250 g (0.55 lb. or 8.81 oz.) small circular pasta
- Parmesan cheese or Greek kefalograviera cheese* to serve

Preheat oven to 190°C (374°F). In a saucepan and on low heat, place the octopus with the bay leaves. Cook, turning on both sides, for about 5 minutes or until it changes color (no need to add any liquid or oil, it should release a little of its own juices). Remove from saucepan. Allow to cool, and cut into bite-size pieces. Discard the liquid that is in the pan.

Using the same pan, sauté the onion in half the olive oil until soft and caramelized. To this, add the octopus and ouzo and allow it to cook out the alcohol (should take around 2 minutes). Add tomato paste, puree, peppercorns, allspice berries, salt, pepper, sugar, cinnamon stick, and rinds. Allow this to cook, covered, on low for around 20–25 minutes or until the octopus is almost cooked. Pour this mixture into a baking dish. Add the remaining oil, pasta, and boiled water. Mix well so that the pasta does not stick. Place uncovered in the oven.

Bake for 25 minutes or until pasta is cooked and liquid has evaporated. Be sure to stir the pasta after the initial 5 minutes in the oven so that it doesn't clump and stick together. This dish must be a little saucy. If it is drying out too quickly, add 1 cup boiled water and mix through. It is best eaten warm. Serve with grated cheese over the top.

*Ouzo liquor and Greek kefalograviera cheese is available at any Mediterranean grocer. Parmesan cheese can be substituted for Greek cheese.

Hot Cheese Dip

Χτυπητή

Serves 5
10 minutes

Hot cheese dip is served throughout Greece as an appetizer. The amount of spice can be adapted, though this dip should be spicy. Some regions don't use yogurt, but rather red capsicums. I have added them below as an option. Adding them will make the dip very red. This recipe is the classically authentic one in tavernas around Athens. It can all be mixed in a food processor, but I prefer a chunkier texture; therefore, use a spoon to mix everything together.

1 hot red chili pepper, whole

½ cup olive oil

1 teaspoon red wine vinegar

1 clove garlic, whole

400 g (0.88 lb. or 14.1 oz.) feta cheese, crumbled

100 g (0.22 lb. or 3.52 oz.) yogurt, strained

1 teaspoon chili flakes

3 red capsicums, roasted and peeled (optional)

Place the red chili, olive oil, vinegar, and garlic in a food processor or use a mortar and pestle (and roasted red peppers, if using them). Pulse until it is all combined and crushed.

In a large bowl, add the crumbled feta cheese, yogurt, chili flakes, and red chili pepper mixture. Gently fold the chili mixture through, mixing to combine well. Refrigerate for 10 minutes before serving.

*Keeps refrigerated for up to 3 days.

Freddo Cappuccino

Φρέντο καπουτσίνο

Serves 1
3 minutes
Gluten-Free

Freddo cappuccino is served in cafes, at beach bars, and in restaurants around the country. In my book *Hellenic Kanella: Memories Made in a Greek Kitchen,* I have a recipe for making traditional Greek coffee brewed on the stovetop in a *briki* and served in small cups. This recipe, however, is what Greeks enjoy in the summer months and when wanting something cold. It features a cold brew with ice and a foamed milk called *afrogalo*.

2 shots espresso coffee

Sugar to taste

Ice cubes

¼ cup whole milk, cold

Cinnamon powder or chocolate powder to serve

First, place your milkshake-maker cup in the freezer. This must be very cold before you begin.

In a tall glass half-filled with ice, add the brewed espresso coffee (add sugar now if you like it sweet). Stir and set aside. Place two ice cubes and cold milk into the chilled milkshake cup and blend using a milkshake maker for 2 minutes or until a thick foam has been achieved. Pour foam into coffee cup. Sprinkle cinnamon powder and enjoy!

Ice Cream Two Ways— Yogurt or Halva

Παγωτό—γιαούρτι η χαλβά

Serves 1
3 minutes
Gluten-Free

Ice cream, or *pagoto*, is a dessert served everywhere in Athens. These two flavors are delicious and easy to make. You do need an ice cream churner. The preparation is simple, and the result is fantastic!

Yogurt Pagoto

450 mL (15.22 fl. oz.) yogurt

150 mL (5.07 fl. oz.) thickened cream (heavy cream)

150 g (0.33 lb. or 5.29 oz.) icing (confectioners) sugar

1 lemon, zested

Honey to serve

Sour cherry preserve* to serve

Halva Pagoto

140 mL (4.73 fl. oz.) runny honey

200 mL (6.76 fl. oz.) whole milk

300 mL (10.14 fl. oz.) thickened cream (heavy cream)

200 mL (6.76 fl. oz.) tahini paste

Honey to serve

Sour cherry preserve* to serve

Place all ingredients (of either yogurt or halva pagoto) into a bowl and whisk to combine. Place into ice cream churner that has been precooling. Churn for 40 minutes or as directed on your machine.

Pour into a container and freeze until set into a scoopable ice cream consistency. Serve either ice cream with honey drizzled over the top or sour cherry preserve.

*Sour cherry preserve available at Mediterranean grocers.

Glossary

All ingredients are available at Mediterranean grocers. Please note that I am not a physician and therefore do not suggest this information to substitute any medical treatment, diagnosis, or therapy.

Allspice berries: A berry that imparts similar notes to cinnamon, nutmeg, clove, and a hint of pepper. It is the dried and ground up fruit of a small berry from the Jamaican bayberry tree. It is also known as pimento. In Greece, it is also known by the name *bahari*. It is used primarily to flavor stews and sauces.

Almonds: Almonds are considered by many a nut but are actually a fruit. The tree bears a fruit that consists of an outer hull and a stone-like seed within. The almond trees grow very well in Greece, especially on the island of Crete. Almonds can be eaten raw, unsalted, baked, or candied. It is a versatile nut in many sweet treats throughout Greece and is high in vitamin E, magnesium, and copper.

Capers: Capers are the unopened flower buds of the prickly caper plant, *Capparis spinosa*, which is native to the Mediterranean region, especially on the island of Santorini. Capers are generally pickled or salted. They add a great burst of acidity and saltiness to food.

Cinnamon: In Ancient Greece, cinnamon, derived from the ancient Greek word κιννάμωμον (*kinnamomon*), was an exceedingly valued spice. Said to have originated in Egypt, it soon became an integral part of the Greek cuisine. The queen of all spices, cinnamon is said to regulate blood sugar and is rich in antioxidants. It is used in both savory and sweet foods.

Cloves: Cloves are the flower buds of the clove tree. They are pungent in flavor and used in both savory and sweet foods. Cloves are high in antioxidants and are known to help kill off bacteria, reduce blood sugar, and promote bone health.

Cornmeal or polenta: Cornmeal is a coarse flour made from dried maize yellow corn and has been cultivated in Europe since the sixteenth century. It is used in pies and/or porridge-like foods.

Cumin powder: Cumin is a flowering plant native to the Middle East and India. Cumin seeds are usually dried, then made into a powder. It is helpful in aiding digestion and improving blood cholesterol and is a great source of iron. It is mainly used in savory foods.

Eggplant: This vegetable is grown in many countries, but in Greece, the *tsakoniki* is the most famous of the heirloom eggplants, a slender, purply-white variety that is narrow and sweet. They are a great source of vitamins and minerals, increase brain function, and help with digestion.

Extra-virgin olive oil: Extra-virgin olive oil is the highest quality of unrefined oil. It is processed without the use of any chemicals and is high in antioxidants. The oil is released from the first pressing of the olives. It is high in monounsaturated fat.

Fava beans: Fava beans are a crop cultivated on the island of Santorini, where the soil, lack of water, and climatic conditions create an exquisite-flavored bean both velvety in texture and sweet to taste. Fava beans are rich in protein and a great source of vitamin B1, magnesium, potassium, and high fiber.

Fennel seeds: These come from the fennel plant and have an aniseed flavor. They are grown all over the Mediterranean and have a great source of fiber and antioxidants and help lower LDL cholesterol.

Feta cheese: Feta is a crumbly, aged cheese commonly produced in blocks. It is a salty white cheese made from Greece's sheep's milk and/or a combination of sheep's and goat's milk.

Filo pastry: Filo pastry is thin, unleavened sheets of dough made from flour and water used for making pies and desserts.

Garlic: A vegetable, garlic is a member of the onion family (*Allium sativum*). Each segment of the garlic is called a clove. It can be eaten cooked or raw.

Grape must (also known as petimezi): Grape vines have been part of Greek civilization since 1700 BC. In ancient Greece, there were several varieties of grape must (or grape juice before being made into wine), depending on the degree to which it was boiled. *Gleukos* was the name of the fully ripe or overripe pressed grapes before fermentation. From this word *gleukos*, we get the word *glucose*. *Hepsema* was the name given to the concentrated form from boiling the must to a thick syrup. In ancient times this was used as a sweetener (and the only one, together with honey) that was added to many breads and desserts due to its intense sweetness.

Honey: Greek honey is one of the most natural nutritious foods, filled with antioxidants and antibacterial properties. The rich variety of Greek flora and the unlimited summer sun have given Greece some of the best honey in the world. Hippocrates wrote, "Honey and pollen cause warmth, clean sores and ulcers, soften hard ulcers of lips, heal carbuncles and running sores." Just maybe he was right!

Kalamata olives: Kalamata olives are only found in the Peloponnese peninsula in the southern region of Greece. They are generally handpicked to avoid bruising. These olives are high in iron; calcium; vitamins A, E, C, and K; magnesium; and potassium. Kalamata olives also contain phenolic compounds, which are natural antioxidants.

Kasseri cheese: Kasseri is an unpasteurized sheep's milk cheese with no more than 20 percent goat's milk mixed in. It is a semihard, white, slightly stringy cheese. This cheese is similar to a mozzarella cheese.

Kataifi pastry: Kataifi is shredded pastry resembling fine strands. It can be used both in savory and sweet dishes. It is best thawed before using.

Kefalograviera cheese: Kefalograviera is a hard, salty, yellow cheese made from Greece's sheep's milk and/or a combination of sheep's and goats' milk. It is a mild- to medium-tasting cheese with air holes spread throughout the cheese. This is recommended for making fried *saganaki*.

Mastiha: Mastiha is a resin derived from the mastic tree, which grows on the island of Chios. It comes in a crystalline drop or in powder form. It has anti-inflammatory and antioxidant properties and also aids in gastrointestinal problems.

Mizithra cheese: Mizithra is a fresh, unpasteurized white cheese made with milk and whey from sheep's, cows', or goats' milk. Mizithra in the context of this book is always the hard-dried variety used for grating over pasta.

Oregano: Two Greek words compose *oregano*: *oros* ("mountain") and *ganos* ("joy"). So oregano means "joy of the mountains." It is a quintessential ingredient for Greek meals. Oregano is a flowering plant from the mint family. It has a slightly bitter taste, yet is warm and aromatic. It has many nutritional benefits, such as calcium, iron, potassium, and vitamin E.

Ouzo: Ouzo is the colorless, unsweetened spirit of Greece. Its flavor profile is anise. It is made by distilling grapes (or occasionally other fruit), then flavored with fennel or anise seeds. It is best served over ice.

Petimezi: Petimezi is otherwise known as grape must and one of the world's oldest natural sweeteners. Petimezi is made by boiling down grape juice in enormous vats for hours and days until only a fifth of the original liquid remains. It is basically a concentrated grape juice. Ensure that you buy an authentic grape molasses without any sugar, color, preservative, or additives added. Petimezi is loaded with iron, potassium, and vitamins A and B. It is used in savory and sweet dishes throughout Greece.

Pistachios: Pistachios are at the very heart of Aegina, an island twenty-seven kilometers from the heart of Athens. It was here that Greek cultivation of pistachios began in 1896, where the plant thrived due to the dry soil. The pistachio tree came to Greece from Western Asia and is part of the cashew family. *Fistiki Aeçinas* are a rare variety that have a pale blonde outer shell, fuchsia-tinged exterior, a nut that is bright emerald when ripe, and a tighter-closed shell, and they are handpicked and dried in the sun for optimal taste. Pistachios are low in fat and high in fiber. They consist of monounsaturated fatty acids and are loaded with antioxidants.

Quince fruit: Quince fruit is part of the Cydonia family *Rosaceae*, which likewise comprises apples and pears, among other fruits. It is most commonly eaten cooked; it also can be eaten raw, though it has a slight furry texture and can be a little tough. Quinces are cultivated where there is a warm climate. The fruit has a tart but aromatic flavor that is released when cooked. Quinces are a great source of vitamins, minerals, antioxidants, and fiber.

Saffron: Saffron is a spice derived from the flower of *Crocus sativus*, commonly known as the "saffron crocus." This spice is among the costliest in the world and is known to have been first cultivated in Greece. Saffron has a subtle aroma and flavor, containing vitamins A, C, and B, along with magnesium, calcium, potassium, and iron. It comes in thread form or in a powder; a mere pinch gives color and flavor to dishes.

Semolina flour: Semolina flour is made from durum wheat and can be ground coarse or fine.

Tahini paste: Tahini is a sesame paste made from 100-percent ground sesame seeds, used extensively in Turkish, Greek, and Middle Eastern cooking. Sesame has been a common ingredient since antiquity in many Ancient Greek recipes. Sesame seeds are soaked in water and then crushed, which separates the bran from the kernels. The kernels are then skimmed off the surface, toasted, and ground till an oily paste is produced, thus the tahini paste. It is a great source of protein, vitamin E, iron, copper, and calcium.

Trahana: Trahana is a pebble-shaped grain made from either semolina, wheat flour, bulgur, or cracked wheat. Milk or yogurt is added to the flour, and once combined, they are broken into pieces, dried, and then broken into the small, pebble-like shape. This porridge-like mixture was eaten by the Ancient Greeks and Romans. It was a practical way of using leftover milk, as refrigeration did not exist. Trahana can be stored in a cool, dry place for up to a year. Trahana is rich in carbohydrates, is a good source of fiber, and aids in intestinal health. It is used in pies to soak up moisture or can be substituted for rice in stuffed vegetables or eaten as a soup.

Yoghurt: *Oxigala* is what the Ancient Greeks called yogurt. It is a type of sour milk, as they would say. Greek yogurt contains good bacteria, which aids in helping digestion.

Index

A

ALMOND MEAL:
Almond and Honey Cookies, 29
Almond and Orange Little Pears, 31
Pasta Flora with Fig Jam, 37
ALMONDS:
Almond and Honey Cookies, 29
Caramel Jelly Pudding with Almonds, 193
ANCHOVIES:
Tapenade (Olive) Dip, 85
APPLES:
Beetroot Salad with Walnut, Apple, Honey, and Yogurt, 225
ARTICHOKES:
Braised Artichokes with Baby Peas, 103
Roasted Goat with Fresh Dill and Artichokes, 98

B

Baked Chickpeas with Rosemary, 173
Baked Eggplants with Garlic Paste, 27
Baked Eggplants with Peppers, 53
Baked Feta Cheese, 72
Baked Patties with Lemon Potatoes, 231
Baked Quince with Spices and Ice Cream, 51
Baked Sardines, 187
Baklava with Shredded Pastry, 121
BEEF:
Baked Patties with Lemon Potatoes, 231
Beef Stew with Quince, Petimezi, and Rosemary, 21
Cheese-Stuffed Veal in Tomato Sauce, 25
Roast Beef with Vegetables and Melted Cheese, 195
Spiced Meatballs in a Lemon Yogurt Sauce, 125
Stewed Aromatic Beef with Eggplant Mash, 65
Venetian Pastitsio, 33
Beetroot Salad with Walnut, Apple, Honey, and Yogurt, 225
Braised Artichokes with Baby Peas, 103

C

Caramel Jelly Pudding with Almonds, 193
CHEESE:
Baked Eggplants with Garlic Paste, 27
Cheese Pie with Shredded Pastry, 127
Cheese-Stuffed Veal in Tomato Sauce, 25
Cornmeal Spinach Pie with No Pastry, 197
Honey Cheesecake from Sifnos, 171
Ricotta Pancakes with Honey, 149
Roast Beef with Vegetables and Melted Cheese, 195
Spaghetti and Cheese Pie, 77
Trahana Pie with No Pastry, 203
Vanilla Pastries, 145
Venetian Pastitsio, 33
Yogurt-Coated Pasta with Caramelized Onions and Cheese, 179
CHICKEN:
Chicken and Chickpea Stew, 175
Chicken Livers with Egg and Lemon, 205
Chicken "Pollo in umido", 43
Roast Chicken with Mandarin, Orange, Honey, and Thyme, 155
Stewed Chicken with Sage and Rosemary, 154
Wine-Cooked Rooster with Egg Pasta, 87
CHICKPEAS:
Baked Chickpeas with Rosemary, 173

Chicken and Chickpea Stew, 175

CHOCOLATE:

Chocolate and Walnut Cake, 111

Chocolate Log with Orange and Honey, 221

Tahini Cake with Chocolate, Honey, and Olive Oil, 227

CINNAMON:

Cinnamon Cordial, 177

Fried Pastry with Walnuts, Cinnamon, and Honey, 81

COD:

Salt Cod with a Potato–Garlic Dip, 19

COFFEE:

Freddo Cappuccino, 239

Cookies with Mahlepi, Mastiha, and Orange, 159

Cornmeal Spinach Pie with No Pastry, 197

Cretan Teas, 152

CUCUMBERS:

Tzatziki (Yogurt and Garlic Sauce), 223

CURRANTS:

New Year's Cake, 185

Shredded Lamb with Currants and Pine Nuts, 181

Custard Pie of Thessaloniki, 59

D

Dakos Salad, 151

Dentrolivano or Rosemary Tea, 152

DILL:

Roasted Goat with Fresh Dill and Artichokes, 98

E

EGGPLANTS:

Baked Eggplants with Garlic Paste, 27

Baked Eggplants with Peppers, 53

Eggplant Salad with a Garlic–Lemon Sauce, 63

Eggplant Spoon Sweet, 55

Stewed Aromatic Beef with Eggplant Mash, 65

F

Faskomilo Tea, 152

FETA CHEESE:

Baked Eggplants with Peppers, 53

Baked Feta Cheese, 72

Beetroot Salad with Walnut, Apple, Honey, and Yogurt, 225

Cheese Pie with Shredded Pastry, 127

Cheese-Stuffed Veal in Tomato Sauce, 25

Cornmeal Spinach Pie with No Pastry, 197

Hot Cheese Dip, 237

Sesame-Coated Feta Saganaki, 117

Spaghetti and Cheese Pie, 77

Trahana Pie with No Pastry, 203

Yogurt and Cheese Pie, 123

FIG JAM:

Pasta Flora with Fig Jam, 37

Fish in Spicy Broth, 39

Fish Soup with Saffron and White Wine, 167

Freddo Cappuccino, 239

Fried Pastry with Walnuts, Cinnamon, and Honey, 81

Fried Snails with Rosemary, 147

G

GARLIC:

Baked Eggplants with Garlic Paste, 27

Eggplant Salad with a Garlic–Lemon Sauce, 63

Marinated Octopus, 229

Roast Beef with Vegetables and Melted Cheese, 195

Roasted Goat with Fresh Dill and Artichokes, 98

Salt Cod with a Potato–Garlic Dip, 19

Souvlaki, 224
Tzatziki (Yogurt and Garlic Sauce), 223
White Fish with Lemon Emulsion, 225
GOAT:
Roasted Goat with Fresh Dill and Artichokes, 98
Grape Must and Orange Cookies, 95
Grape Must Pudding, 93
Greek Yogurt Panacotta with Honey, 219
GREENS:
Wild Weeds with Lemon and Olive Oil, 157
Grilled Octopus, 182

H

HALVA:
Ice Cream Two Ways—Yogurt or Halva, 241
Tahini Cake with Chocolate, Honey, and Olive Oil, 227
HONEY:
Almond and Honey Cookies, 29
Beetroot Salad with Walnut, Apple, Honey, and Yogurt, 225
Chocolate Log with Orange and Honey, 221
Fried Pastry with Walnuts, Cinnamon, and Honey, 81
Greek Yogurt Panacotta with Honey, 219
Honey Cheesecake from Sifnos, 171
Ice Cream Two Ways—Yogurt or Halva, 241
Ricotta Pancakes with Honey, 149
Roast Chicken with Mandarin, Orange, Honey, and Thyme, 155
Tahini Cake with Chocolate, Honey, and Olive Oil, 227
Hot Cheese Dip, 237

I

ICE CREAM:
Baked Quince with Spices and Ice Cream, 51

K

KASSERI CHEESE:
Baked Eggplants with Garlic Paste, 27
Roast Beef with Vegetables and Melted Cheese, 195
KEFALOGRAVIERA CHEESE:
Cheese Pie with Shredded Pastry, 127
Cheese-Stuffed Veal in Tomato Sauce, 25
Roast Beef with Vegetables and Melted Cheese, 195
Spaghetti and Cheese Pie, 77
Trahana Pie with No Pastry, 203
KEFALOTYRI CHEESE:
Cornmeal Spinach Pie with No Pastry, 197
Venetian Pastitsio, 33
Yogurt-Coated Pasta with Caramelized Onions and Cheese, 179

L

LAMB:
Shredded Lamb with Currants and Pine Nuts, 181
Slow-Cooked Lamb and Potatoes in Baking Paper, 129
Lazy Wife's Bougatsa, The, 41
LEMONS:
Baked Quince with Spices and Ice Cream, 51
Baked Sardines, 187
Chicken Livers with Egg and Lemon, 205
Cinnamon Cordial, 177
Eggplant Salad with a Garlic–Lemon Sauce, 63
Eggplant Spoon Sweet, 55
Grilled Octopus, 182
Ice Cream Two Ways—Yogurt or Halva, 241
Marinated Octopus, 229
Olive Oil Spiced Pie, 130
Pork and Celery Stew with an Egg and Lemon Emulsion, 99
Revani (Yogurt and Semolina Cake), 69

Roast Chicken with Mandarin, Orange, Honey, and Thyme, 155

Roasted Goat with Fresh Dill and Artichokes, 98

Salt Cod with a Potato–Garlic Dip, 19

Spiced Meatballs in a Lemon Yogurt Sauce, 125

Spinach Risotto, 91

Split-Pea Puree with Caramelized Onions from Santorini, 169

White Fish with Lemon Emulsion, 225

Wild Weeds with Lemon and Olive Oil, 157

LIVERS:

Chicken Livers with Egg and Lemon, 205

M

MAHLEPI:

Cookies with Mahlepi, Mastiha, and Orange, 159

MANDARINS:

Roast Chicken with Mandarin, Orange, Honey, and Thyme, 155

Marinated Octopus, 229

MASTIHA:

Cookies with Mahlepi, Mastiha, and Orange, 159

Milk Pie with Homemade Filo Pastry, 113

Mountain Tea, 152

Muhallebi - Milk Pudding, 61

MULLET:

Pan Fried Red Mullet, 183

N

New Year's Cake, 185

O

OCTOPUS:

Grilled Octopus, 182

Marinated Octopus, 229

Octopus Stew with Pasta, 235

OLIVE OIL:

Olive Oil and Orange Cookies, 83

Olive Oil Spiced Pie, 130

Tahini Cake with Chocolate, Honey, and Olive Oil, 227

Tapenade (Olive) Dip, 85

Wild Weeds with Lemon and Olive Oil, 157

OLIVES:

Tapenade (Olive) Dip, 85

ONIONS:

Baked Chickpeas with Rosemary, 173

Baked Sardines, 187

Cornmeal Spinach Pie with No Pastry, 197

Fish in Spicy Broth, 39

Fish Soup with Saffron and White Wine, 167

Octopus Stew with Pasta, 235

Roast Beef with Vegetables and Melted Cheese, 195

Souvlaki, 224

Split-Pea Puree with Caramelized Onions from Santorini, 169

Stewed Chicken with Sage and Rosemary, 154

Yogurt-Coated Pasta with Caramelized Onions and Cheese, 179

ORANGES:

Almond and Orange Little Pears, 31

Chocolate Log with Orange and Honey, 221

Cookies with Mahlepi, Mastiha, and Orange, 159

Grape Must and Orange Cookies, 95

Marinated Octopus, 229

New Year's Cake, 185

Olive Oil and Orange Cookies, 83

Roast Chicken with Mandarin, Orange, Honey, and Thyme, 155

Souvlaki, 224

Spiced Tahini Baklava, 233

OREGANO:

Rigani or Wild Oregano Tea, 152

P

Pan Fried Red Mullet, 183

PARMESAN CHEESE:

Cornmeal Spinach Pie with No Pastry, 197

PASTA:

Octopus Stew with Pasta, 235

Spaghetti and Cheese Pie, 77

Venetian Pastitsio, 33

Wine-Cooked Rooster with Egg Pasta, 87

Yogurt-Coated Pasta with Caramelized Onions and Cheese, 179

Pasta Flora with Fig Jam, 37

PASTRY:

Baklava with Shredded Pastry, 121

Cheese Pie with Shredded Pastry, 127

Custard Pie of Thessaloniki, 59

Milk Pie with Homemade Filo Pastry, 113

Sesame Pie, 213

Spaghetti and Cheese Pie, 77

Spiced Tahini Baklava, 233

PEAS:

Braised Artichokes with Baby Peas, 103

Split-Pea Puree with Caramelized Onions from Santorini, 169

Stewed Sweet Peas, 101

PEPPERS:

Hot Cheese Dip, 237

Pickled Hot Peppers, 57

Pork Stew with Peppers, 106

Spicy Stew of Peppers, Sausage, and White Wine, 207

PETIMEZI:

Beef Stew with Quince, Petimezi, and Rosemary, 21

Grape Must and Orange Cookies, 95

Grape Must Pudding, 93

Pickled Hot Peppers, 57

PINE NUTS:

Shredded Lamb with Currants and Pine Nuts, 181

PORK:

Pork and Celery Stew with an Egg and Lemon Emulsion, 99

Pork Stew with Peppers, 106

Souvlaki, 224

Spicy Stew of Peppers, Sausage, and White Wine, 207

POTATOES:

Baked Patties with Lemon Potatoes, 231

Fish Soup with Saffron and White Wine, 167

Roasted Goat with Fresh Dill and Artichokes, 98

Salt Cod with a Potato–Garlic Dip, 19

Slow-Cooked Lamb and Potatoes in Baking Paper, 129

White Fish with Lemon Emulsion, 225

Q

QUINCES:

Baked Quince with Spices and Ice Cream, 51

Beef Stew with Quince, Petimezi, and Rosemary, 21

R

RED MULLET:

Pan Fried Red Mullet, 183

Revani (Yogurt and Semolina Cake), 69

RICE:

Spinach Risotto, 91

RICOTTA CHEESE:

Cheese Pie with Shredded Pastry, 127

Honey Cheesecake from Sifnos, 171

Ricotta Pancakes with Honey, 149

Vanilla Pastries, 145

Rigani or Wild Oregano Tea, 152

Roast Beef with Vegetables and Melted Cheese, 195

Roast Chicken with Mandarin, Orange, Honey, and Thyme, 155

Roasted Goat with Fresh Dill and Artichokes, 98

ROSEMARY:

Baked Chickpeas with Rosemary, 173

Beef Stew with Quince, Petimezi, and Rosemary, 21

Dentrolivano or Rosemary Tea, 152

Fried Snails with Rosemary, 147

Souvlaki, 224

Stewed Chicken with Sage and Rosemary, 154

S

SAFFRON:

Fish Soup with Saffron and White Wine, 167

SAGE:

Faskomilo Tea, 152

Stewed Chicken with Sage and Rosemary, 154

Salt Cod with a Potato–Garlic Dip, 19

SARDINES:

Baked Sardines, 187

SEAFOOD:

Baked Sardines, 187

Fish in Spicy Broth, 39

Fish Soup with Saffron and White Wine, 167

Grilled Octopus, 182

Marinated Octopus, 229

Octopus Stew with Pasta, 235

Pan Fried Red Mullet, 183

Salt Cod with a Potato–Garlic Dip, 19

White Fish with Lemon Emulsion, 225

SESAME SEEDS:

Olive Oil and Orange Cookies, 83

Sesame Bread Rings, 49

Sesame-Coated Feta Saganaki, 117

Sesame Pie, 213

Shredded Lamb with Currants and Pine Nuts, 181

Slow-Cooked Lamb and Potatoes in Baking Paper, 129

SNAILS:

Fried Snails with Rosemary, 147

SNAPPER:

Fish Soup with Saffron and White Wine, 167

Soup with Trahana, 201

Souvlaki, 224

Spaghetti and Cheese Pie, 77

Spiced Meatballs in a Lemon Yogurt Sauce, 125

Spiced Tahini Baklava, 233

Spiced Walnut Cake with a Vanilla Custard Topping, 209

Spicy Stew of Peppers, Sausage, and White Wine, 207

SPINACH:

Cornmeal Spinach Pie with No Pastry, 197

Spinach Risotto, 91

Split-Pea Puree with Caramelized Onions from Santorini, 169

STAR ANISE:

Baked Quince with Spices and Ice Cream, 51

Stewed Aromatic Beef with Eggplant Mash, 65

Stewed Chicken with Sage and Rosemary, 154

Stewed Sweet Peas, 101

T

TAHINI PASTE:

Ice Cream Two Ways–Yogurt or Halva, 241

Spiced Tahini Baklava, 233

Tahini Cake with Chocolate, Honey, and Olive Oil, 227

Tapenade (Olive) Dip, 85

THYME:

Roast Chicken with Mandarin, Orange, Honey, and Thyme, 155

TOMATOES:

Baked Chickpeas with Rosemary, 173

Baked Eggplants with Garlic Paste, 27

Beyond the Greek Salad

REGIONAL FOODS FROM ALL AROUND GREECE

Ruth Bardis

"Let food be thy medicine, and medicine be thy food."

— Hippocrates